50 Years in the Sport

Javier García Cuesta

Dedication

"This book is dedicated to my lovely wife Linda whose love, support, encouragement and hard work allowed me to have a wonderful career in handball. Without her, none of this would have been possible."

CONTENTS

Javier García Cuesta
JESÚS LÓPEZ RICONDO

The fighter that Javier García Cuesta always was, wants to leave us his sporting experience in this book that he wants me to prologue. I don't know the reason Javier asked for my collaboration on this project. One can never know the reasons why we make certain decisions. Was it the friendship two displaced persons from the north of Spain developed once they found each other in Madrid? Or maybe the feelings and emotions they shared while representing Spain in a faraway country. Perhaps it had to do with the respect that I always had for his technical decisions when I was President of the Spanish Federation.

Javier's beginnings in handball were in the Colegio Corazón de María de Gijón, training with his very dear coach José Antonio Roncero. We met when he was a player for Club Atlético de Madrid.

After he became a teacher of Physical Education, the club gave him the opportunity to work with professional fútbol teams (Atlético Madrileño and the First Team) as Conditioning Coach under the supervision of coaches Luis Aragonés and Joaquín Peiró.

After four years of work, he moved to the USA and began his journey of becoming, perhaps, the most prolific coach of handball national teams of all time.

In 1981, he started working with the USA Men's Team preparing for the 1984 Olympic Games in Los Angeles. They were a competitive team, and some of the players played in European clubs. After the role ended in 1987, he returned to Spain.

We followed his signing with Teka Santander very closely, and two years later he was hired by the Spanish Federation as Technical Director and Coach of the Men's National Team. So when I became President of the Spanish Federation,

Javier was already there. I kept him in the position because I was convinced of his technical skills.

It was before the Barcelona '92 Olympic Games, when he was working with twenty players and he needed to cut four. We had a difference of opinion, but concluded with cutting the four players from Catalunya.

The decision was totally the coach's opinion, it cannot be any other way. I let him know this decision could bring us a lot of criticism, and that's exactly what happened.

We did it his way, and we both had to assume the consequences which caused some pain.

In 1995, he signed with Egypt which was preparing for the 1999 World Championship with players like El-Attar and a generation of young players who were junior World Champions two years before.

In 1999, he went to Portugal, and in 2005, he returned to Spain as Technical Director. In 2008, he went to Brazil to continue the good work that Jordi Ribera had started.

Finally, the USA Federation called him again and he started a program at Auburn University (Alabama) with young players hoping to carry the flag into the future. If this happens, it is probably because of the seed that he planted in Auburn.

Allow me to pass on to you some of the ideas or advice he gave during his years of work:

"Planning and training is as important as the competition. We have to be ready because you never know when the opportunity will come. Pay attention to the player that 'knows' everything, he could be a distraction from the instructions of the coach."

"My biggest accomplishment was to be able to be in handball, become a full-time worker in handball, and build my life from 1968, when I became independent of my parents, until 2018 when I retired."

Maybe the absence of Linda, his wife–who was probably more Spaniard than he–moved him to write and describe his multiple experiences in international handball, which hopefully can be used by the new generations of our sport.

MANUEL GARCÍA DE LA CÁMARA

As President of the Asturian Handball Federation, it was a pleasure to receive a call from Javier García Cuesta in reference to a publication describing some of the history of our sport. My friendship with Javier goes way back, and even though we live parallel lives, we always find each other in handball.

Asturias is part of the identity of our country, a land and people where origins take roots that allow us to understand our history. All this is reflected in Spanish handball, where Asturias holds a prominent position.

The Asturian Federation was founded on October 17, 1957, to take care of all the handball activities that would take place among our beautiful towns and landscape.

From then until today, all kinds of experiences, anecdotes, and multiple individual and group stories have formed and built Asturian handball–turning it into an iconic sport.

Here we know each other. It is difficult to forget some names. Who doesn't remember Villamarín's moves, García Cuesta, or Juan de la Puente wearing the captain armbands of the national team, and later on the Entrerríos brothers, Ruesga, Garabaya. Who can forget the celebrations of Jessica Alonso after she scored the last goal in the historic Bronze Medal Game with the Guerreras.

But to get there, the clubs are very important, for example: La Calzada, Gijón Jovellanos, Grupo Covadonga, Avilesina, Base Oviedo. The Asturian Federation represents all the organizations and entities that work every day for the development of our players.

If we are talking development, Asturias should be very proud of some coaches who got us to where we are today. Allow me to name one of the best: Javier García Cuesta, handball player with the Atlético de Madrid, Conditioning Coach with the club's First Division fútbol with Luis Aragonés as a First Coach, national team coach for Spain, but also with the USA, Egypt, Portugal, and Brazil.

Handball was very lucky Javier became interested. Now that so much emphasis is put on information data, we are missing the humanism and personality Javier possesses. He has knowledge, is a studious innovator, and is always attached to the land where he grew up.

The fact a person like Javier wanted me to write a prologue for his book, is not only a proud moment for me, but also a responsibility with a friend who wants to describe his personal experiences during his professional trajectory.

Thank you, Javier, for letting me be part of this piece of work that I am sure will be a motivational element for all those that consider formation an everyday part of their lives.

MICHAEL D. CAVANAUGH

Former National Team Player
Former National Team Coach
Former CEO of USA Team Handball
Competition Director of Handball for the 1984 Olympic Games
Competition Director of Handball for the 1987 Pan American Games
Competition Director of Handball for the 1990 Goodwill Games

When Javier García Cuesta first entered the USA Team handball family in the late '70s, we were experiencing daunting challenges at virtually every level. We had little structure, little funding, we suffered in obscurity from a lack of exposure and promotion, and recruiting/retaining elite athletes was one of the most pressing issues. What Javier brought to our struggling program was discipline, enthusiasm, and professionalism both on and off the court. His impact on the players he inherited throughout the years was nothing less than legendary!

He quickly became what we refer to in the American sports psyche as a "player's coach"–meaning the players would do anything for him. He instilled in them a desire to play for one another and to reach their full potential along with a goal to strive to exceed even their own expectations.

His training methods were grueling and demanding, but always in line with what is the essence of what one encounters in a handball match. While he was a disciplined taskmaster, he encouraged clever, creative thinking and play in match situations. He was a master technician capable of taking existing talent and blending the players into a cohesive unit with a "giant killer" mentality!

Javier was also a master and passionate motivator. His analysis of an opponent's strengths and weaknesses led to tactics and match plans that were stellar. USA players came from a wide variety of other sports and one early impression of our athletes on Javier was how hard they were willing to train, work, and sacrifice to have the opportunity to wear the USA jersey and represent their nation! Javier knew how to channel this asset. A rare few can boast of such high level of success on multiple continents, with multiple national teams within multiple cultures and multiple international competitions!

Success is often measured in wins and losses, but Javier transcends this level of assessment by way of his style, manner, and positive impact that are his enduring qualities, and that he has left so many with lasting impressions. I know that readers will enjoy learning about Javier's thoughts and reflections of his very unique career. I remain profoundly grateful for having Javier in my life, and for what he has given to the world of handball. I am proud to know him as a friend and brother!

INTRODUCTION

I am very satisfied after finishing this book because at least two of the main goals I set out with, have been accomplished:

1. To give back to Asturian handball some of the many honors and distinctions they gave me throughout all these years. Actually, I never worked in Asturias, and when I competed there, it was as a Coach of the other team in a friendly or official match, I also came to complete courses or clinics. I even had the honor of being the Coach of the Men's Asturian Team.

I thought the best way to accomplish this would be to tell what I did, and all the experiences I went through, and hope some of them could be useful for the new generations of coaches.

My advice to them is, if you find something that you like or something that you can use, don't hesitate to use it but always adapt it to your work, to your reality, and apply it in a way that is best for your circumstances. In one statement: *Make it yours and remember that there is no better lesson than what we learn when we think we know everything.*

2. To recognize and thank all the people, coaches, teachers, teammates, officials, managers, family, and friends who taught me all I know and gave me an opportunity. Also the players and people of different fields who formed my staff, who made my job possible and made me a good coach.

Handball has developed and the quality of the game has improved. Television adds a new dimension to it with more cameras, different angles, slow motion, etc. Considering all of this, handball is now a good show, and we all should be trying to maintain and improve it, making sure that the work we do is the best it can be.

It is our responsibility as coaches to make sure we do our best job with the team that is competing at an optimum level in our organization and obtaining the best possible results. But it is also our responsibility to have new players ready to substitute and take the place of the older ones when the team and the organization needs them.

In Spain, like most of the countries in Europe, all this is done through the clubs by finding and developing new players who—when they reach the top—will be involved with the national teams after they are selected among the best in the country.

The Spanish Federation, through the Base Program (Detection of Talent), does a very good job detecting talented athletes and teaching them when they are still young (13-14 years), and the same when slightly older (15-16 years).

But we are still lacking, after so many years of telling the officials of the need for a similar program to prepare and improve those players when they are juveniles (17-18) and juniors (19-20).

It has to be a program that combines school responsibilities with the sport's needs. They need to go to school in those years, but we need to find a way that gives them the possibility of training some extra hours which will complement the time and work they do in the clubs.

It is not that difficult if we have the willingness. We only have to copy what France and Denmark do. They have the best programs to develop juveniles and juniors. The results, when they are adults, are very obvious. We have to look at the results in the Olympic Games and the World Championships.

Some of you are already doing that work in the clubs and in the young national teams. Thank you for your work, and thank you for your service developing players, and improving the team, and handball in general at all levels.

Keep it up and *always go forward no matter what.*

REASONS WHY I WROTE THIS BOOK

For a long time, I debated whether it would be worthwhile to compile all the information, experiences, and situations I had to face during my sports career.

There were so many years—fifty to be exact. Yet, I finally decided it would be a good idea to collect all this information, organize it, and shed some light on why some decisions were made, in addition to how all the pieces of the puzzle fit together and how they are connected to each other.

It won't be easy to put myself in the first person talking about other people, taking the chance of putting them in a difficult position, or expressing their opinions the wrong way. It never was and never will be my intention to hurt or undervalue anyone's beliefs.

Seriousness is contagious

I never thought of doing this when I was working because it could have been taken as an excuse or for self-interest.

Now the situation is different. I am not working anymore, and I don't have the attachments to any institutions that could have prevented me from saying certain things. Only the discretion and the principles inherent to my profession may condition my statements or discussions.

To pass information is part of our progress

The generations pass, culture stays

The following are the main reasons why I wrote this book:

- To thank and celebrate the teachers, coaches, managers, family, and friends who were involved in my education and who helped me grow into the person I am. This includes for sure the players and people on my staff in the different places I worked. Also, I would like to acknowledge the presidents and managers who gave me such great opportunities.

  - To pass on information, ideas, advice, and explanations of how I reacted, and how I planned my way through the challenges I faced during all the years. I hope what I share will be useful for the next generation of coaches.

  - To relieve myself of feelings that have been accumulating out in the open. I wanted to explain "my side of the story" by giving my opinion, and clarifying the reality and circumstances that revolved around those events, important jobs, and tasks I had the honor to take part in.

  - It was a very constructive way of spending my time now that I am retired. I do miss the time, schedule, and routines involved in the practices, games, and their preparations.

PROFESSIONAL TRAJECTORY

I was born in Mieres (Asturias, Spain), and I lived there until I was fourteen years old. Like any other kid, during school vacations I would play soccer all day with a break to go home and have lunch. One of those years they organized a handball tournament in the city schools. I went to see some games because my brother was playing on one of the teams as a goalkeeper. This tournament was my first contact with handball.

In 1961, my family moved to Gijón, and we lived across the street from Colegio Corazón de María, so the decision of what school I would go to was very easy. I started the next school year and completed three years.

One day in Physical Education class, the teacher organized some handball games after he asked if anyone had played the game before. I told him I knew the game and played before—which was not true, I only watched my brother's games.

After we finished the first game, the teacher (José Antonio Roncero) asked me to play the next game. When we finished, he told me he wanted me to train with the school team. Of course I said yes, and that's when and where everything began.

Final Against SAFA

CODEMA Infantile

I played on the team throughout my time in school (infantile, cadet, juvenile). This was the beginning of everything. During those three years I competed with Asturian Selection and participated in some tournaments and games with Algodonera de Gijón. Once I finished Codema school, I attended the University of Oviedo, studying Physics for two years. I was very attracted to the world of sciences; it was the time of the Space Race, NASA was founded, etc.

On the weekends I went home and trained with teams in Gijón and also with the Algodonera de Gijón Adults Team.

Cantabric Games

Youth Codema

Asturian Selection

Important Day to Get to Know Domingo Bárcenas

After two years in Oviedo, I realized my studies in Physics and the so-called "Modern Mathematics" were not my strongest points. I made a decision to change studies and move to Bilbao to attend the College of Economics at the University of Bilbao. My plan was to finish with handball and become a normal student of Economics. I wanted to forget my time playing handball. I wanted to stop playing and dedicate myself to study—with the blessing of my parents who were paying my tuition plus the cost of room and board in a boarding house near the school.

Two events changed the course of that plan:

1. Roncero, my coach, wanted me to play with the school team (Codema where I finished high school) for a National Championship. He called me and I told him that I was finished with handball, and I didn't want to play, which made him very upset, ending the conversation. Sometime after, I received a call from my parents saying Roncero asked them to convince me that I was an important player on the team and should go to the National Championship. My father—who was a simple man who believed in laws and rules—promised my coach he would talk to me. I was very upset because I didn't think my coach should have gone around me talking to my parents, "negotiating" my participation in the tournament. Finally, I returned to handball until the end of the tournament.

2. When I was in Bilbao, I got the news there was a División de Honor game upcoming. It was Salle Beyena against Granollers. I never saw a First Division game before. It was played at La Salle High School. There were no stands, only a bunch of people behind the lines. I went behind the officials' table in order to hear the coaches talk.

   When the game ended, I was listening to both teams, wondering if I should ask for an autograph, but I didn't have the courage. All of a sudden, the La Salle coach looked at me and our following conversation went like this.

   "What are you doing here?" the coach asked. I looked around to find no one else and he then said, "You are García Cuesta, right?"

   "Yes," I said.

   "What are you doing here?"

   "I came to watch the game."

   "No, what are you doing here in Bilbao?"

   "I am studying in Deusto in the Facultad of Economics."

   "Tomorrow we have practice sometime in the evening. I want you to come and play with us."

   He knew me from the Cantabric Games I played with Asturias. He was the Coach of the Basque Team. I couldn't believe what

just happened. I went to the boarding house, thought about it,
and decided to go. Next day, I was a player of La Salle Beyena of
División de Honor (First Division).

These two events were decisive in my career in handball. If it wasn't for the
breaking of my relationship with Roncero and Mr. Herreros, the Coach of La
Salle, showing interest in me, my career in handball would be a veterans game
with my friends, and I wouldn't have the opportunity to write this book.

I played one year in La Salle Beyena. It was 1967, and at the end of that season
I was called for the national team, and from there to the Atlético Madrid, where
I played until 1976. The move to Madrid didn't help my studies of Economics
in Bilbao. The first two years I studied and attended some classes in Madrid, and
then went to Bilbao for exams.

I didn't do very well. I realized I was not going in the right direction, plus handball and sports in general became a very important part of my life. I was independent from my parents, but I became a professional handball player more for my dedication than for the money I earned. Atlético paid for my apartment and I received 2000 pesetas a month. Not a lot, but it gave me good motivation and confidence to dedicate my life to sports. I started my studies in the INEF (Institute of Physical Education) in Madrid. Combining the INEF with my activity as handball player in Atlético Madrid. Also, I was selected for the national team for which I played sixty-five international games. Among those, the Olympic Games in Munich, 1972, and the World Championship in East Germany in 1974.

TECHNIQUE

In 1973, I was married to my American girlfriend, Linda Perrotta. In 1974, our son Carlos was born.

As a new couple raising a family, I decided to take on extra work. I completed my studies and inquired about work at Club Atlético Madrid and continued to play on the handball team. By this time, they increased my salary because I was married but they stopped paying for my apartment.

First International Game Elda

Olympic Team Munich '72

Men's National Team

I had a meeting with Vice President Mr. Salvador Santos where he agreed to inform me of what he learned after he consulted with the people in charge. A few days later they contacted me and I met with Victor Martinez Technical Secretary of Soccer and Paquito the coach. Paquito started in the summer where he became the coach of Atlético Madrileño, second professional football team in the club.

In the meeting, they offered me the job of Conditioning Coach of the Football Team (Atlético Madrileño). I was very happy when accepting the position, and in July, 1975, I began work during pre-season mornings and evenings. Later on when the season started (September) it was cut to only afternoons 4:00 p.m. to 6:00 p.m.

When football training finished around 6 p.m., I had to rush to Magariños Gym to practice with the handball team from 7:30 p.m. to 9:30 p.m. It was like that every day of the week and on the weekends I would go traveling to play with the handball team.

Last International Game (Alicante)

One of my first encounters with Maximov

Club Atlético Madrid Professional Soccer Team

Everything went well. I was very happy with my relationship with Paquito, (one of my idols, when he played in Oviedo FC and Valencia CF), and I enjoyed working with him in soccer. Great professional and good friend.

Time was passing by, and I was getting used to the tight schedule, especially in the evenings. It was around October–November 1975, when a new situation came along and shook all my plans and broke all my molds. One day Paquito called me and told me Luis Aragonés and Joaquín Peiró wanted to have lunch with both of us, so the next day here I was, sitting at a nice restaurant, eating with the three "fútbol-ers".

During the meal, Luis Aragonés told me he and Joaquín would like me to be the Conditioning Coach of the First Team of the club, the Atlético de Madrid Professional First Division Team.

Obviously, I accepted, and the following week I was working with the First Team from 10:00 a.m. to 12:30 p.m. in the morning, 4:00 p.m. to 6:00 p.m. in the afternoon with Atlético Madrileño, and at night 7:30 p.m. to 9:30 p.m. training with the handball team, while also traveling on the weekends to play handball with my team.

We did this from October 1975 to June 1976. At that time, I retired from handball and continued working only with soccer as a Conditioning Coach with the First Team. I signed a contract for the next three years where I worked until 1979.

Those four years were amazing because I had the opportunity to work with prestigious and important coaches. They were an extraordinary source of knowledge, which allowed me to go inside the world of soccer as a sport where I became familiar with the personalities, egos and special interests that generated a Professional Elite Soccer Team. These were the stats of the team during the four years I worked with them:

SEASON	STATS
1975 – 1976	Champions of the First King's Cup
1976 – 1977	Champions of the League
1977 – 1978	Quarter Final European Cup
1978 – 1979	Finished my job in June 1979 and left

The first two years were successful, the other two not so much. My work and my motivation began to decline, and my relationship with some of the players also began to deteriorate. All these things started to make me think that if everything were to continue that way, I'd have some problems, so I decided to look for new challenges.

Champions Spanish League '76–77

Conditioning Work

During these four years, I disconnected totally from handball. I was only involved and dedicated to soccer. I tried to get to know as much about the sport as possible. I took the Coaching Course of Juveniles, and the following year, the Coaching Regional Course. In addition to those education courses, I went back to the INEF to do the two-year Master Soccer Certificate.

Conditioning Work

I finished my work with Atlético in June 1979, but three months before, in March 1979, I went to the USA one week (three days in NY and four days in Los Angeles) because my wife and I already decided that we would move to the USA where I hoped to find a job in soccer after I finished with Atlético.

Thanks to Luís Pereira I got an interview with Professor Mazei in Manhattan. He was in charge of Pelé soccer camps for children. Prof. Mazei offered me an opportunity to work on the camps that summer. After three days in NY, I went to LA where my friend Ray Thorton (tennis instructor and professor at University of California at Irvine) arranged several interviews for me in the area. One of them was with the Manager and Coach of the California Surf (professional team of the American League). We talked and they showed interest, but they didn't make a decision until September.

There was another meeting with two directors of a health club near Los Angeles. As we conversed about my situation over lunch at the club, I realized after plenty of talking—with my not very good English at that time—that the handball we were talking about was not the handball I was thinking of.

Once we clarified that point, the manager remembered, sometime ago, a guy came to talk to him about starting a handball club. He gave my friend Ray the phone number of that person, Mike Cavanaugh, who was Coach of the Men's National Team.

After I returned to Spain, my friend Ray sent a recommendation letter to Mike; to which Mike responded saying he was only the men's coach, but he would forward my letter to the president of the USA Federation, Dr. Peter Buehning.

Around one month later, I received a letter from Dr. Buehning, offering me the position of Coach of the Women's National Team, which was going to help prepare the team for the qualification for the Moscow Olympics in March 1980. The program was to begin training in August for three weeks in the Olympic Training Center in Squaw Valley (California) and then go to Romania and Bulgaria to play in a tournament in each country.

Once again, this was one of those circumstances that helped me without me doing anything. Dr. Buehning was the Coach of the American Team in the Olympic Games in Munich (1972). He remembered me from the Spanish Team; although, I was only in two matches because of an injury. The matches were the "Famous Spain–USA"—which we lost—and the last one was against Tunisia.

At the end of July of 1979, my family and I were in Los Angeles. The situation was like this:

1. During soccer, I waited for the club, California Surf, to give me an answer on the job opportunity which wouldn't be until September. In the meantime, the coach of the team also had a soccer camp for kids, and he offered me a job in the camp that July, which I accepted and worked there all month.

2. In handball, I had the opportunity of working with the Women's National Team during September for three weeks to prepare to go

to Romania and Bulgaria, and after competing in those locations,
the team would go to train at the Colorado Springs Olympic
Center until March 1980, for the qualification in Congo against
Congo and Korea.

Women USA Team

In August 1979, I stayed with my family in the dormitory of Irvine University. I
didn't want to take the chance and wait for the soccer club to make the decision in
September, so I took the offer of the Handball Federation and became the Coach
of the Women's National Team.

That was the end of my soccer adventure and the beginning of my career as
a handball coach. An important moment in my life personally and professionally.
I worked with the Women's National Team until March of 1980. We played the
qualifications in Congo, but we didn't qualify, and finally the USA boycotted the
Moscow Games.

When this happened, both national teams went home and stopped the daily
training. In April 1980, I became Technical Director. My job was to do clinics,
courses, visit clubs and train, and look for possible new players. Parallel to all this,
we started a serious discussion about preparing, planning, and finally executing a
program which would allow the men's and women's teams to train every day and
develop a schedule of games starting in Canada and after, going to Europe three
to four times a year.

The Federation made the decision to move forward with a year-round program in July of 1981. We all went to New Jersey and rented two houses—one for the men and one for the women. The players would go to school at the universities in the area, or they would work during the day, and we would practice at night from 8:30 p.m. to 11:30 p.m. in a military facility in Fort Dix.

I started the program coaching both teams from July 1981 until January 1982, then the Federation hired a Czechoslovakian coach for the Women's Team and went to the Olympic Training Center in Lake Placid, New York. I stayed with the Men's Team in New Jersey.

This program was implemented and executed from July 1981 until the Olympic Games in Los Angeles, 1984.

We practiced every day from 8:30 p.m. to 11:30 p.m. at night Monday to Friday, resting Sunday, and Saturday morning we would do some running outdoors. Two or three weekends per year we went to Canada (Quebec and Montreal).

Leaving Friday afternoon when they finished classes, we would drive to Quebec, play Saturday and Sunday. We then would return Sunday after the games, driving back to New Jersey, arriving around two or three in the morning in order for the team to be able to go to school or work on Monday morning.

Later, we started going to Europe and playing games or tournaments in different countries against clubs or national teams on a very tight schedule, playing eight or ten games in two weeks (the record was fourteen games in seventeen days).

Women's National Team

Concentration Pose

For three months (April, May, June) before the Olympics in LA, we went to Europe and played, and also trained in different countries in Europe. We visited Austria, Slovenia, Italy, Romania, Germany, France, and Spain.

The programs of the national teams (men and women) from July 1981 to the LA Olympic Games 1984, were—without any doubt—the best preparation programs the USA Federation has implemented thus far.

The results at the Olympic competition shows the two teams were competitive, and for all of us who had the honor of participating, it was the experience of our lifetime. For me, it gave the opportunity to learn and become a better coach and a better person.

We will get back to more details when we talk individually about each important event we participated in.

Once the 1984 Olympics were finished, the players went back to their ordinary lives and the program continued, periodically having training camps, preparing for some of the Pan American competitions and the qualification for the B World Championship in Norway in 1985, and Italy in 1987, for both the Men's team and the Women's team.

During this period 1984 until 1987, we also did tryouts, and most importantly attended the National Sports Festival every year, where we found new players. But the core of the team were the players that participated in the program in New Jersey and the 1984 Olympics in Los Angeles. With this new group and the training camps and competitions we mentioned before—especially the W.C. in Italy, where we had a very good performance—we were ready to play the Pan American Games the summer of 1987—which was the Qualification for the Seoul Olympics in 1988.

Men's National Team

We won the competition in Indianapolis against Cuba, in front of 6000 people. It was a great moment for everybody in USA handball and a victory for both teams (men and women).

It was also their respective Qualifications for the 1988 Seoul Olympics, the perfect ending to an excellent job, executing the program that we started in 1981.

Those eight years were full of good and bad. Many happy days together along with some frustrating ones, because we felt so close to the top but still missing that extra push that would put us on the same level as the world's top competitors. The lack of competition experience was without any doubt our Achilles heel, compensated by our team's heart and soul.

For some time before the end of those eight years working for the USA Federation, I had an increasing feeling of "swim, swim and die at the shore."

Plus, some personal and family circumstances once again put me in a situation where I had to choose between:

1. Remaining in the USA, sending all the players home, finishing the programs of the national teams, and maybe two years from then starting all over again. This would mean finding new players, setting up a program to train them, and hoping that this next time I would have a better situation, so you "swim, swim, but you don't die at the shore."
2. Use all of the experience and networking I gained throughout my experiences from all over the world (mainly in Europe) to find a job in the big leagues and prove to myself that I could do it.

It was not easy, and took me some time, but as I said before these two points, the family and personal moments, and for sure the generous offer I received from the club in Spain heavily influenced my decision.

I made the decision around two months before the Pan American Games which was the end of my contract. One month before the games I spoke with Dr. Buehning and informed him of my decision—he and I were the only ones who knew about it. The night before the Final, I informed the team's staff.

Winning the gold medal was an exciting, wonderful feeling, which made it a lot more difficult for me to announce it at the celebration dinner. To beat Cuba and qualify for the 1988 Olympics—I still have the faces of some of the players in my head and I am sure they can see mine.

TEKA Santander

This was the time when I ended my eight years of work for the USA Federation and began my return to Spain working for Teka Santander in the First Spanish Handball League.

My contract was for two years and the family—although very happy for the return to Spain—had to go through moving from our house in Colorado to renting an apartment in Santander.

Our children had to adapt to a new school system, and it was not easy for them even though we put them in a bilingual school the first year.

My adaptation to my new team, new mentalities, new players—better players than the ones I was working in the States—was not easy either.

My methods, the intensity, and attitudes I was used to were not there. I also did not have the same relationships with all the players. It took some time before the level of commitment and quality of work reached an acceptable performance level necessary to play in the Spanish League.

My ignorance and lack of good information about the other teams in the League were resolved by my weekly meeting with my good friend, Luis Morante. He offered and I asked him, even though he was not officially an assistant coach.

When I signed the contract, the planning and design of the team was already finished as far as hiring players, training schedule, preparation games, etc.

However, it was the work, understanding, attitudes, and everyone's efforts that successfully got us through the season. We were a competitive team and finished at the top.

The second year was different—the club mentality changed, and the budget increased, we also had good teamwork, network and coordination between directors, coaches, and even local press. We were able to put together a very strong team with the signing of: Mats Olsson, Christian Arason, Francisco Melo, Javier Cabanas, and Chechu Villaldea. Plus Julián Ruiz, and Luis García were able to form a group of new, talented, local players.

It was a special year for the development of the team. We finished second in the League and were Champions of the Cup against Barcelona. This victory was the first successful accomplishment of the team that invoked great feelings and excitement in the city. It was the beginning of a long list of future victories during the following years that put the Teka Santander team among the best in Spain and Europe.

Not everything was perfect. We ended the season very well in regard to results, but there were some moments when my way of thinking was not the same as others.

I began to have an increasing desire to work with national teams again. I felt that I preferred the more focused and short periods of time, working with a selected group of players, and making them play well as a team in specific competitions instead of long seasons like from August to June.

King's Cup Champions

To add to all this, my wife and I were not very happy with the schools our kids were attending in Santander. We wanted them to follow the American system. This would also make it easier when they ultimately attended college in the USA, which was our intention.

After some time, we decided to go back to the US where my wife found a job as a teacher and I found more work in sports.

A few weeks before the end of my contract and the end of the season, I spoke with the club explaining our intention of going back to the US as soon as we finished the season. We ended with the King's Cup.

The team ended on a very high note and we were initiating our move to Colorado Springs, where we had a house rented, and we were confident we would be able to find employment with our network of people.

In the middle of all this, one day I received a call from D. Antonio Zamorano, General Secretary of the Spanish Handball Federation, saying he wanted to talk to me.

When I went to Madrid, I had a meeting with D. Antonio Zamorano and the President of the Federation. They offered me the position of Technical Director and Coach of the National Team for the next four years—which included the Olympic Games, Barcelona, 1992—I accepted. The family and I moved to Madrid. When we settled in, our children attended the American School of Madrid and my wife was able to get a job in the same institution, which made it a good situation for us as a family.

Working Group

In July 1989, I initiated my work as a Coach of the Men's National Team of Spain with two games against Russia in Leon, and the rest of the summer assisting Cruz María Ibero, Coach of the Junior Men's National Team, preparing for the Junior World Championship in Galicia.

The next three and a half years I was totally dedicated to preparing the national team for the Olympic Games in Barcelona '92. It was going to be a special chapter dedicated to executing the plan we designed and agreed upon.

We finished in fifth place, and for some people it was a disappointment. For others, including me, we finished in the same position as the Olympic Men's Team had so far in the Olympic Games and World Championships. We also renewed the team and added some players from the junior team. This became the core of future national teams.

Working Group

First European Selection 1993

During 1993, I had the honor of being nominated as the Coach of the First European Selection, celebrating the creation of the European Federation.

Shortly after, I searched for a new job. I was presented an offer to work at a club in Tunisia, but ultimately I declined the offer.

The Suisse Federation in Zurich also showed interest, however, we weren't able to come to an agreement. Therefore, I was in the same situation again: Should I look for a job in Spain, or should I look outside?

The option of going to the States was again possible—our son was studying at Central Michigan University. We planned a trip to the US with two objectives. We visited future universities for Cristina, and we checked on job opportunities for Linda and me. For that we scheduled a meeting with Dr. Buehning in Short Hills, New Jersey.

We arrived at Dulles Airport in Virginia. Linda's brother was waiting for us to take us to his house where we stayed a few days. When I called my parents to tell them we arrived safely, my sister-in-law informed me my father passed away due to a sudden heart failure while preparing breakfast.

The critiques and commentary around the Barcelona Olympics were something my father was not prepared for. It caused him to have episodes of anxiety and depression that to this day I am convinced accelerated his death.

I canceled the meeting with Dr. Buehning, changed the tickets, and the next day, went back to attend my father's funeral.

Close to all these events—around two months before the League finished—I received a very attractive offer from Teka. We had a meeting and we agreed for me to be the coach of the team for the next two years.

Sadly one of the most negative episodes of my career as a coach occurred. Still to this day, I believe I should have done more.

With only two months left in the competitions, Teka's team was very skilled and the results were also good. I was surprised they wanted to hire me under these circumstances.

I asked what the situation was with Emilio Alonso—the coach at the time. The answer was Emilio will not be the coach next year. Then I asked who is going to inform him, the answer was, "We are."

I began to prepare to move to Santander. I already finished my job with the Federation, the moving, the care for my mother—whose health needed some attention—and my father's death made it a little more difficult.

The fact was the communication with Emilio was not done, and the announcement of my new position created a very tense situation in my relationship and friendship with Emilio. It took some time before it went back to normal as it remains today.

I should have contacted Emilio on my own, but ending my role with the Federation, my father's death, my mother's health, the stress of unemployment, etc. caused me to have a very defensive attitude and a desire to forget everything. I wanted to get to Santander, get involved with my team and forget all the other things that were related to recent work.

All of this is fine, but I signed a contract with a club that still had a coach, and what was worse, Emilio was my friend. I am not very proud of my decision at the time and even at this moment, years after, it's still present in my mind.

In the summer I started the pre-season with Teka and after, we started the League.

The team was very strong with the addition of very good players like Talant Dushevayev, Yakimovich, and Mateo Garralda. Great team, great players, better structure behind the team, very good support from the crowd—the gym practically full every game—and very extensive press coverage, mostly favorable of the team by the media (newspapers, radio, and television).

However, some weeks passed and the team didn't play well. The results of the matches in the League and in the European competitions were not as expected, so clearly things were not right. The players were nervous and filled with a lot of anxiety. I started having individual meetings, team meetings with players, and management including the president of the club.

All this brought me to the conclusion that we were facing a typical scenario where there is a high-level team with good players, but also big egos. These players all had different backgrounds, different cultures and nationalities with different philosophies and understandings of the game. And most importantly, they weren't used to different ways of dealing with cultures outside of their own.

I spent close to two months trying to find solutions, typically technical, tactical work where I used different players in different positions and changed strategies. Sometimes things got a little better, but when we came to the game, the performance and results did not coordinate with the quality of the team. The crowd placed pressure on all of us—players and coaches—expressing their disappointment with the situation and the way we were playing.

Parallel to this work, I continually spent a lot of time and energy meeting with the players, directors, and the president of the club, looking for the answer to all these questions and problems.

After more than a month, I had a clear idea of what was going on. Like I said before, combining groups with different ideas, attitudes, and learning processes, along with their egos and different experiences, didn't make a very good combination.

Nonetheless, it was my job to fix this. That's what the coaches do, and that's why they hired me.

After I gathered all this information, I set up a big meeting with the whole team. Gratefully, it was a success. It was very productive and honest, and the players expressed their feelings and opinions, and allowed us as a team to clarify all the positive and negative situations.

At the end of the meeting, I was very pleased with the outcome, many good and direct recommendations and promises were made. The final commitment was to make an honest effort to change the situation we were in, and we agreed the team as a whole was more important than the individuals.

We left feeling good and very optimistic, but the happiness didn't last very long. The next morning all the newspapers exposed everything that was said in the meeting.

As you can imagine, the next game at home was—if I had to describe it—I would say horrible and also interesting. I realized my job and work wasn't bringing in the best results. Also, my mental state was not very good. I was convinced I didn't have much more to offer and decided the best solution was to resign. We needed to change something that would calm the situation in the games and allow the quality of the team to show up.

Clear understanding is always important

Support from above is important

At the end, it had to happen.

I met with the directors of Teka and came to an agreement to resign and break my two-year contract. At this point it is fair to say I do not have the words to express my gratitude and appreciation to the people responsible for Teka (D. José Casuso and D. José Antonio Revilla) for their support and understanding throughout the process.

It was now the end of 1993, beginning of 1994. The postponed phone conversation with Dr. Buehning occurred and ended up with my nomination as Technical Director. The U.S. Federation had made the decision of starting a similar program to prepare for Atlanta in 1996—same as the program we created in New Jersey when we prepared for Los Angeles, 1984.

My job was to oversee all the things that happened around both mens and womens teams such as finding places for practice, organizing tryouts, searching for new players, and increasing the social network that would eventually help us later on.

Both teams had their own coach: Claes Hellgren with the women, and Vojtech Mares with the men.

Overall the conditions for practice were okay, but like always there were some difficulties. We were training at schools at night, and the players would go to school or work during the day.

Some months passed, training was progressing well, but I saw tension growing between the Federation in New Jersey and the organizers in Atlanta. One million dollars were raised from the Weather Channel (part of CNN). This money—which under normal circumstances should be beneficial for everybody (program, players, coaches)—became the source of friction.

At the same time, there were elections for President of the Federation. The opposition to Dr. Buehning argued that there were too many foreign coaches around the teams. Another very important fact is that some people wanted Dr. Buehning out of the President position even after years of work and dedication. So when elections were held, Peter Buehning lost.

The winners took a strong position against the foreign coaches. Vojtech Mares was the first to leave, then it was my turn to decide if I should stay or if I should go.

Finally, I was out, but first I had to go to the World Championship in Iceland, 1995, with the Men's Team. We practiced for three weeks and after, headed to the championship. During the tournament, once again a game-changing event happened that gave me the opportunity of coaching the National Team of Egypt.

This was a quality jump in my career returning to the handball elite, and also it was happy times for my family. My wife ended up teaching in the American College of Cairo, and Cristina, our daughter, attended the same institution.

We got to know some of the executives of Repsol, the Spanish oil company, which was very helpful for us. We spent a lot of evenings enjoying their company and friendship—very good people. For me with all the traveling it was a sense of security knowing that Linda and Cristina were in good company.

Cristina was at an age where she could be influenced by her environment. She got very involved in the culture and traditions of Egypt, and it was definitely her introduction to the Arabic world that she now loves so much with her husband and family.

She did very well at the American College of Cairo, and her speech as Students' Representative at the Annual Graduation Ceremony in front of the pyramids was a very special moment for my wife and I.

Back to handball, during the Iceland '95 Championship, I watched a game of the team we had to play the next day and all of a sudden Dr. Hassan Moustafa (at the time, president of the Egyptian Federation) sat next to me. I knew him from a meeting we had the year before in Italy with the Algerian coach, where we discussed the open defense.

We were watching the game and talking when he asked me about the American Team, and I explained after the Championship I would be looking for a job. At that moment he said they were not satisfied with the German coach they had and after the Championship they would be looking for a coach.

I asked him if I could give him my resume since I could be interested. He said yes. Luckily I had my resume with me to provide him with a copy. The next day at the games, I gave it to him and he said they would get back to me in a couple of weeks.

I went back with the team to Atlanta, and a few days later I got a phone call from the General Secretary of the Egyptian Federation offering me the position of Coach of the National Team. Days later, I accepted, and was given my new contract and a ticket to Cairo.

The Players Atlanta 96

Also, when we were in Iceland, I had conversations with a French TV commentator about coaching the Paris Saint-Germain team. We were friends since we played against each other when we were juniors in the Latin Cup.

Once again, I was at home in Atlanta sitting at my desk and actually had two offers to consider coaching a club team or coaching a national team.

The decision was easier this time. The offer of coaching the Egyptian National Team for one year and being at the Olympic Games in Atlanta '96 was a lot more attractive, so I packed up and went to Cairo. Linda and Cristina would join me one month later.

The Officials

Pharaohs in action

Gohar Nabil

It was Summer of 1995, when I went to Cairo. I knew the team since we played against them a few times before. I knew that it was a good team with good players, and it was surprising to discover we would be training at the Olympic Training Center.

It had an amazing handball court, weight training room, Olympic track and field stadium, and very pleasant and comfortable dormitories next to good quality restaurants.

I received a lot of help and support from the Federation, and also the Olympic Committee, the Ministry of Sports, and from high government institutions.

With all the support, there were very high expectations, and the planning and objectives were very ambitious, pointing to the top of international handball.

National TV and media outlets didn't waste any time. They traveled with the team and extensively covered any news concerning the team to the point of broadcasting every game. The streets of Cairo were empty and everybody was at home watching the game.

The work on the court was good. The players were used to hard work, and discipline was never a problem. They assumed the responsibility, and veterans and new players were very aware of the bonuses for victories.

The national team players in Egypt were what we would call *professionals*. The money they received from their club added to the money received for the national team. It was for sure above the salary of any average worker in Egypt.

In Egypt, there is an interesting League with two teams in Cairo of good level (Zamalek, Ahly) playing in Alexandria and Port Said. The League played games on Friday. The players rested Saturday and Sunday, but Sunday evening we met at the training center in Cairo. We practiced Monday and Tuesday morning and evening. After, the players went to the club's practice on Wednesday and Thursday to play again on Friday. We maintained this program practically the whole year plus.

Every three or four months we went to Europe to play games and tournaments. Also, we had to play the Official African Championships, which are Qualifications for World Championship and Olympic Games.

The time I was in Egypt, we played these competitions in: South Africa, Benin, Tunisia, and Zimbabwe. Also, we played at the World Championship in

Kumamoto, Japan, 1997 where we finished sixth, the same maximum result the team got in the World Championship in Iceland, 1995.

We executed this program in 1995–1996 and participated in the Olympics in Atlanta, 1996. We finished sixth, which was the best result so far for Egypt in the Olympiad.

At the end of the Olympics in Atlanta, my contract was finished. The team returned to Egypt. I stayed until the end, and the president also stayed. We watched some games together. We had a chance to talk, and through these conversations we had an agreement that I would remain as coach of the team for three more years until the World Championship in Egypt, 1999.

The next three years, as I mentioned before, were very pleasant and happy times for my family, with my wife teaching and my daughter attending classes at the American School in Cairo. We enjoyed the company and the quality time we spent with our friends from Repsol, including the times that we were invited by the Spanish Embassy to some receptions and parties.

Atlanta Opening
Ceremony

Suez Canal

This good family situation and my job situation also had some tense and difficult moments, which was kind of normal when you consider the high-profile, responsibility and media that was associated with the position. The players in general accepted such a responsibility, but there were also some tough moments where the performance of the team was affected.

Some other situations also had influence. It was the fact that some people in the Federation were not expecting me to renew my contract three more years and extend my work until 1999 when we would play the World Championship in Egypt. Maybe they had different ideas.

The first two months of my work after the Atlanta '96 Olympics were a difficult time, with a lot of meetings with the people in charge of the control and approval of the programs related to the national teams.

It was an interesting time for me as a coach to be sitting at home discussing and deciding who would be my assistants in my staff group, what kind of schedule to use for preparation and most importantly what kind of systems we should use on offense and defense.

Lots of time was dedicated to deciding the kind of defense we should use. It was for me a very testing experience being there with old ex coaches, explaining my methods, and arguing if we should defend close, zone defense, or a more open individual defense. We compromised and agreed that we should be defending a bigger zone in a 3–3 system.

This system combined, the help and togetherness of any zone defense (in this case over a bigger area) with the more individualistic work against the opponents, and most importantly against the ball that the players and officials were more familiar with. We added a weight training program to strengthen the 1:1, and I had to get used to having my defenders at 10–11 m returning when necessary to the 6–9 m situation. I have to say that after some time it was very encouraging to see the players moving and enjoying the work.

Besides the big responsibility and tensions that were inherent to the job, I was very proud of having the opportunity of working with these players and officials, and most of all working for and with Dr. Hassan Moustafa. I am grateful to him because he not only hired me, but also defended the program in the good and the bad moments, and supported the independence of the program that we designed and approved without allowing any interference or any situation that could be negative for the team.

In thinking about the work we did in the four years I was in Egypt, there will be certain episodes that I am sure will be useful for coaches. Some of them could be difficult to understand with our mentality, and you as coach have to assume the responsibility and redirect the program.

A few examples include:

- We had to punish an important player and suspend him from training, traveling, and playing on the team, and stop his salary for six months.
- Deciding when is the best time to train during Ramadan when the players cannot eat or drink anything from sunrise to sunset.
- Losing a game against Israel in a friendly match in a tournament in Holland. The anxiety that was produced for the players and officials, to the point that one of the officials on the bench, without telling me anything, went on the court and stopped the game. You can imagine the explanations I had to give the Federation to tell them what happened.
- Figuring out what to do, when six months before the World Championship they fire you from your job to put in another coach, and fifteen days later they tell you that you have to come back to the team after you already arranged everything with your next opportunity once you finish the work in Egypt.

The World Championship was in July 1999. My contract would end right after that. I had an agreement with Portugal that when the World Championship ended and my contract would finish in Egypt, I would go to work in Portugal. When they removed me from the team, I spoke with Portugal asking them when I should start. They said immediately, so we started planning our move to Portugal. I would go first, and my wife and daughter would go later after they were finished with school. So, when Egypt called and said that I had to go back to the team, I had to call Portugal explaining what happened and said that I wouldn't be able to go to Portugal until the end of the World Championship in July.

Everything fitted much better this way. Cristina was able to graduate in June, Linda was able to finish her work at the school, and we all headed to Spain when I finished my job with the Egyptian Federation. First to rest for a couple of weeks, and then Cristina went to George Mason University in Virginia, USA, and my wife and I went to Lisbon.

Communication

Egypt

This offer to coach the Portugal National Team came from many conversations and meetings with Dr. Luis Santos, president of the Portuguese Federation. Also, I had several conversations with Professor Carlos Cruz concerning the possibility of me working in Portugal. Finally, it looked like everything was falling into place.

I was very happy returning to Europe and having the opportunity of working with the Portuguese Federation. Dr. Luis Santos, the President, is one of the most intelligent persons I ever met in the handball world.

His ideas were without any doubt the most concrete and practical that I had ever heard in any handball meeting. There were some about how to make handball a prosperous business. He was also one of the people that gave me and my family the best treatment.

The work with Professor Carlos Cruz was also very pleasant and formative. He had good knowledge of handball, and was always trying to combine handball with the professional world.

The other person that I had a very close working relationship with was Dr. Henrique Torrinha, manager of the office. He helped me a lot with my work in the day to day, also introducing me to all the local handball communities all over the country, especially when we were doing clinics, tryouts, conferences, etc.

These three people were very important in my job in Portugal. The Federation worked and had a structure similar to the Federations in the rest of Europe, but there were two things that surprised me. One was the quantity of agreements and protocols that they signed with the regional federations, city halls, clubs, etc. The other thing was the mentality of buying the buildings, offices, etc. where all the regional Federations were working instead of paying rent.

Preparing 2003 World Championship

The National Team program, like most of the European Federations, was based on the work of the clubs adding some training camps during the year, preparing for Qualification, and participating in all the official competitions.

The plan that I presented to the Federation, and was approved, included more training camps. That meant more working time. At the beginning we did some work on the 3–3 open defense for two reasons.

1. Coming from Egypt being used to this kind of defense, I wanted the team to be ready to play against this kind of defense. It was a hot topic—an open debate about this defense—and many teams were using it.

2. I think that we improved the 1:1 which was a good thing for us when we went to a closer, traditional defense (6–0, 5–1, 3–2–1, etc.).

I worked for six years in Portugal. The first two were very good and the team was able to get the best results. The only problem was that the expectations went too high and we got a lot of coverage in the media.

There was also much anxiety and concern whether the facilities for the World Championship would be ready.

Portugal Team

Information before work

The last two years were a bit difficult. The tense relationship between the clubs and the Federation got worse and worse.

There were some meetings (clubs–Federation) to create a professional league. At the last moment the clubs did not accept the conditions that the Federation was proposing and decided to do it separate from the Federation. This started a very big confrontation which at first looked like the annual argument between the parties, but developed into a political problem, and was sometimes very personal against Luis Santos.

All this formed a very negative effect on the work of the national teams to the point that some clubs banned the players from attending the training camps of the national team. This only got worse, when the media was involved. TV and newspapers had a field day.

I believe that the bad performance during our World Championship also had an influence and didn't help soften the dialog. On the contrary, it added some more wood to the fire which lasted a few months.

The last straw was an interview with one of our good players who questioned my silence and requested a public statement explaining my point of view and telling what side I was on.

I had a very clear idea of what my point of view was and tried to influence and change some people's minds, but I didn't think I should be doing it publicly on the TV or the radio or papers.

It was clear that the solution would take a long time, and people would have to accept different opinions and points of view. Professionalizing handball is only possible if we have sponsors, or other money outside of the simple and normal development of a League, or the punctual, sporadic, and short period of time of the Olympics or World Championships.

It is only possible if all groups can do their parts (Federation, clubs, Olympic Committee, Ministry of Sport, television, regional governments, city halls). This way handball can compete in the market with other sports, especially on television.

In the years we are talking about (2000–2005), all this was only possible in a few countries: Germany, Denmark, and Norway, only in certain competitions, and for sure Portugal was not one of them.

If all the institutions mentioned in the parenthesis above would work together, and each would contribute to the limit of their possibilities, and give to the greater project, "professional handball," will work.

Extra effort is necessary

PORTUGAL JOGA COM SUÉCIA E ITÁLIA ANTES DO «PLAY-OFF» PARA O EUROPEU

Cumprir ciclo vitorioso

Entrevista de JOSÉ LOPES

GARCIA CUESTA, seleccionador nacional, está a preparar com todo o cuidado a tentativa de apuramento de Portugal para o Europeu da Suécia do próximo ano. Como objectivo imediato há que ultrapassar no play-off a Holanda. Pela primeira vez o técnico espanhol fala deste adversário e do planeamento que preparou para os dois jogos com os holandeses. Mas García Cuesta vai mais longe e comenta ainda as entradas de Mats Olsson e Manuel Laguna na equipa técnica nacional, assim como os desabafos de Aleksander Donner.

um dos melhores adversários que nos podia calhar.»

A tempo e horas o técnico espanhol preparou esta fase de apuramento cujos pormenores não se escusou a divulgar. «Tudo está dependente das equipas que vão participar no play-off final do Campeonato em que os dois jogos terão lugar a 11 e 15 de Maio e o terceiro, se necessário, a 19. Dessa forma o programa está preparado para a meio do mês de Maio começarmos a trabalhar com uma equipa B que irá treinar e efectuar dois jogos, em Portugal, frente à Suécia, a 19 e 20 de Maio. Depois está previsto que no dia 23 se juntem os restantes jogadores. Começaremos a trei-

We qualified for all official competitions

JAVIER GARCIA CUESTA, seleccionador de andebol

«Há que trabalhar m[...]

Daniel Ribas

JAVIER García Cuesta é seleccionador nacional de andebol desde o seu [...]

«Nenhuma equipa é campeã sem um bom guarda-redes. E há quatro jovens identificados, para serem sujeitos a um programa especial»

Internacional player 1+1=3

Also, it is important they make sure the management of clubs and Federations are done responsibly and all are mindful of their expenses (players' salaries, coaches and staff, directors and president, public relations, promotion and marketing, management and maintenance of the facilities, control of the attendance to the games, and number of tickets sold).

In short, we should not think "what teams we want," but rather "what teams can we support?"

We can have all the amateur and recreation teams we want if we are able to put together all the elements needed. Generous people are able and willing to help others, and dedicate their time, effort, and in many cases money to develop and run the practices and competitions. Congratulations and thank you to all the people dedicated to that noble cause. You are the base of handball. That's the reason we called it "handball base."

That applies also to the lower regional and national competitions. A professional handball league must be sustainable in the short and long-term. Like any company or business it must report profits, carry manageable debt and plan prudently for the future.

More than one time we had this conversation with Dr. Luis Santos, Carlos Cruz, Henrique Torrinha, and I before and during the confrontation which lasted several months. I liked their opinions very much. I am still convinced the organization that Luis Santos wanted to form with the clubs would make a difference having the ingredients necessary for the beginning of a professional competition.

I never saw in any of the Federations that I worked, the connections and number of protocols, agreements, and pre-contracts between the national Federation and the regions and local communities in Portugal.

His great relations, network, and personal friendships with the international and national Federations have convinced me that the entity he wanted to form would be a sustainable, efficient example to follow for other countries.

With this in mind, when I saw that the conflict was beginning to bother the work of the national team, that's when I decided that I would leave at the end of the season. I talked to Luis Santos. He understood my reasons and we only had to get to June. The rest was not my war.

Well, I think we already talked enough about the negative points, so I want to talk about the strengths of Portuguese handball.

1. Portugal has good organization at all levels. The people in charge are responsible, serious, and do a good job.
2. I was very lucky to work with the best generation of players so far.
3. The Federation was able to get the resources to support the strategic plan that we presented, increasing the number of training camps and friendly competitions. The good work done in the clubs combined with the plan put the team at a very good level of performance.
4. I don't want to forget to say that one of the strengths of the Portuguese National Team when I arrived was the tactical quality thanks to the work done by the clubs, and especially the work done by Donner in Sporting Braga.
5. We managed to qualify and play all the official championships held in those five years:

EUROPEAN CHAMPIONSHIP CROATIA 2000
WORLD CUP FRANCE 2001
EURO SWEDEN 2002
WORLD CUP PORTUGAL 2003
EURO SLOVENIA 2004

6. We had some great victories against teams such as Serbia, Norway, and Czech Republic.
7. The performance and work of the entire Federation to organize, develop, and achieve the objective at the IHF Congress in Lisbon 2000, was excellent.
8. We organized the World Cup in 2003.
9. We decided to hire Manuel Laguna as coach of the Junior National Team, and Mats Olsson as goalkeeper coach and my assistant. This team staff structure is one that many teams talked about but could not form. We were pioneers of what is now totally normal on most teams.
10. We created a strategic plan of daily work for juniors with a very clear intention.

11. I had worked with Mats as a player in my Teka days, and I knew I would bring knowledge and experience to the goalkeepers, but I also trusted his personality, work habits, and professionalism that I knew would help the Portuguese players.

12. We selected two groups of juniors: one in Lisbon under the leadership of Manuel Laguna. We trained in the mornings (two hours) and combined their studies, work, and training with the clubs for the rest of the day.

Some of these players later became part of the national team. The duration of the program was one year and was interrupted because it was very expensive. This coincided more or less with the beginning of the problems with the clubs. I am convinced that if there had not been that distraction, the extra money that was needed would have appeared, and the patience necessary for a program like this to bear fruit and produce that "special generation" would also have been present.

As for Manuel Laguna, I had not had the opportunity to work directly with him, but I had very good references and the daily work with him was a great advance in my training as a coach.

Manolo is one of the best coaches I have met, both in training players as well as in preparing coaches with his presentations and theoretical talks and practical sessions, leaving behind him a trail of professionalism and good work for all the countries where he has worked.

My next move was to go back to Spain as Technical Director of the Spanish Federation. It happened like this:

In 2004, the Asturian Federation organized an event in Avilés to which I was invited, and which Jesús Ricondo also attended. We had the opportunity to talk, and in the conversation, he asked me what my plans were. I told him that once my contract with Portugal ended (June 2005), I would not continue and I would look for another job.

He told me that if he were to be elected president again, he would like us to work together as coach and Technical Director. Jesús and I had known each other for a long time.

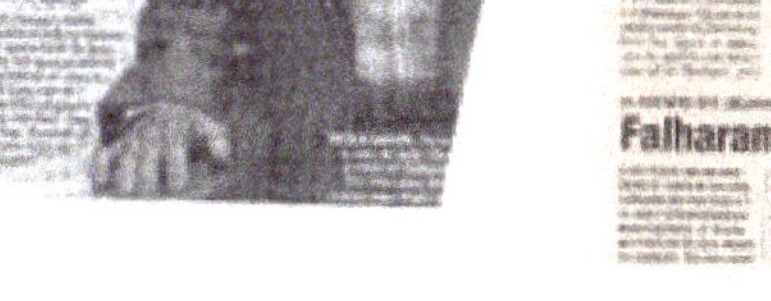

Motivation is always a priority	*Gratitude*

When he was elected president of the Spanish Federation after the resignation of Mr. Roberto Tendero, he confirmed and assumed the contract that I had signed with the Federation until 1993. In a word, our professional relationship over the years became friendship, not only between him and me, but also our families.

This is where a new factor appears. He knew that Carlos, my son, had studied Physiotherapy at Central Michigan University, and was working in Washington. His plan was to study in the USA and return to Spain, and in the past we had discussed the possibility that one day Carlos could work in the Federation.

Returning to the event in Avilés and the conversation in which he told me that if he were to win the election, he would offer me the position of coach and Technical Director, and also offer me the possibility that Carlos could work for the Federation. I was pleased to have this potential opportunity and very happy that my son could possibly come to Spain which was his biggest dream.

I had to finish my contract in Portugal, and there were several months left. When I returned home to Lisbon, I commented and discussed the pros and cons of the offer with my wife, and we called Carlos in the USA. The ceilings of my apartment in Oeiras were not high enough for the jumps we all made.

I talked to Jesús, accepted the offer, and I went back to Lisbon to finish my contract in Portugal. As I said before, I spoke with Luis Santos and informed him of my decision, and we started as a family the preparations to go to Madrid (sale of our apartment, search for a house in Madrid including one where Carlos would live with us until he became independent, moving, etc.).

Jesús won the elections, time passed, and there was not much time before the World Championship in Tunisia in 2005. The Federation hired Juan Carlos Pastor to direct the national team in that World Cup.

Juan Carlos Pastor did a phenomenal job and the team played very well. To everyone's joy, for the first time, Spain was proclaimed World Champion in handball, but also played in a way and with strategies in attack that the players performed exceptionally, and in defense confirming the new trends that had developed. This type of play changed the concepts and fundamentals of defending not only against the opponent, but also the ball with interceptions and deterrence. A lot of risks were taken, but it also created a lot of problems for the other teams.

When everything ended and the celebrations and deserved recognition was over, Jesús called me and we met in Madrid. He told me he believed Juan Carlos Pastor should continue as the head of the team, and offered me a position as Technical Director, but not national coach.

I totally agreed and accepted the position of Technical Director first because I really wanted to work again at Ferraz 16. Second, because it could help Carlos fulfill his dream of working in Spain.

In the summer of 2005, I started my work in the Federation, and one of my first actions was to meet with Juan Carlos Pastor in Valladolid because we did not know each other well. Among many other things, we talked and established the lines of work between the two of us such as if I wanted or would be interested in dictating guidelines that should be followed by all the national, junior, and youth teams for which the Federation is responsible.

Juan Carlos replied that each team had its coaches and that they should be independent. We agreed on this, and from that moment and the next three years our contracts lasted, the Men's National Team acted independently of the Technical Commission that I directed, and Juan Carlos Pastor and his staff were fully responsible for it.

Logically the Federation and the Technical Commission were in charge of logistics and bureaucracy (money, travel, hotels, etc.).

Teamwork

Proud Father

I started my work in the Federation alternating my time in my office in Ferraz sixteen with visits to the training sites and the work of the Junior Women's Team in C.A.R. of Sierra Nevada.

Carlos came to Spain, lived with us in Majadahonda, and joined the group of physiotherapists of the Federation. He participated in the training site in Sierra Nevada, and later joined as a physiotherapist working with the Men's National Team in preparation, and later in competition in the European Championship in Switzerland 2006.

Carlos worked hard trying to integrate in all aspects, and for months he looked for different work options. He left home in Majadahonda around seven in the morning to open a clinic in Alcobendas that he shared with a colleague and they combined their schedules. Carlos worked from 8:30 a.m. to 5:00 p.m.

Then he went to the Alcobendas club where he attended the lower and women's sections from 6:00 p.m. to 9:00 p.m. He came home around 10:30 p.m.

During all this time he realized that the world of physiotherapy in Spain was very different from the one he knew in the USA, and after a year he decided to return to the USA where he currently lives and works.

The years 2005 to 2009 were spent in my case alternating bureaucratic work with visits to the practical activities that were happening, and I would highlight the following accomplishments:

1. Cooperation agreement with Denmark at the level of the basic categories (cadets). A Danish teacher/coach would come and work in our training site, and a technician of ours would go to Denmark to do the same job. It was carried out in the cadet training, and Professor Petersen, director of one of the academies where Denmark works with its rising stars visiting Spain; and in return, I went to do a clinic in Denmark to present our talent detection work.

2. The agreements were signed for the creation of the Men's Scandibericos Tournaments that would be held each year between the national youth teams of Norway, Denmark, Sweden, Portugal, and Spain. It was to be held each year in one of the countries, alternating one year in Scandinavian countries, and the next in the Iberian Peninsula, Portugal, or Spain.

3. The same agreements had already been signed for the Women's national youth teams some time before.

4. Special attention was devoted to the Women's National Team introducing changes at all levels: change of coaches, staff, and cast of players, introducing younger players into the team, and taking advantage of a good generation that had been developing.

5. The regional program for children throughout the country called "Nanobalonmano" was aimed at younger children. It was created with a separate budget from the normal Technical Commission and contributed entirely by the Higher Sports Council.

6. The good work of logistics and support that had always been provided by the Technical Commission of the Spanish Federation to the junior and youth teams (male and female) was continued.

7. A lot of energy was devoted to collaboration and efforts to bring to fruition the negotiations to integrate the School of Coaches into the university.

The good relationship with the Spanish Olympic Committee was maintained and strengthened, which greatly favored the logistics and preparation for the Beijing Olympics. For the Beijing 2008 Olympiad, including the trip we made in 2007, with Federations to inspect the facilities (Olympic Village, transportation, services) and exchange activities with the Chinese Federation. In the case of handball, we had matches against the Chinese Women's National Team in Spain.

Tiananmen 2007

Olympic Working Group

Once these activities were highlighted, it only remains to say, I enjoyed and always considered it a pleasure to work with the employees of the Spanish Federation and to carry out the work and function of our National Federation.

As time passed, so did the 2008 Olympiad, and the end of my contract approached. Signs and details of the strategies of different groups seeking power in the Federation were becoming evident. That meant a new election for president would occur. It would be between Juan de Dios Román, and the standing president at the time, Jesús Ricondo. This time Jesús did not catch me off guard as he did in 1993. I saw it coming. I did not want the politicking and actions people take during elections to catch me flat footed, nor did I want it to affect me or my family.

For a long time, I had a relationship with the Brazilian Federation and specifically with its president Manoel Luis Oliveira. We had known each other since we met during the Pan American Championships held in Manaus 1983, when Manoel Luis was president of the Brazilian Federation as well as organizer of the Pan American Championships.

Since then, whenever we met in competitions, or in IHF congresses, or symposia, the conversation arose that I had to go to train in Brazil. I had the opportunity several times to give clinics, and I had the opportunity to meet many people in Brazil with whom I had and have a great friendship.

When the Portugal thing happened, Luis Oliveira once again contacted me and insisted that I go there. I explained to him the reasons why I went to Spain and that going to Brazil had to wait. However, with the Spanish Federation elections pending, I decided to cover my back in case there was a change in the presidency. Manoel Luis and I agreed that in case of change, I would go to Brazil.

I want to clearly express that I did not have any problem with Juan de Dios. Simply, the games of power and movement of chairs never were things that attracted me. I never liked them, and I always tried to stay away from them. I think Juan de Dios counted on me and the knowledge I had. He was very surprised when we informed him I was going to Brazil. We spoke to inform him of what we were doing during the Technical Commission.

After the resignation of Juan Carlos Pastor—once Beijing 2008 was finished, we had to play the Qualifiers (2 games of Qualification for the European Championship against Ukraine and Malta) before the elections. The Federation very sharply decided these matches would be led by an interim coach, and after the elections, they would appoint the permanent coach. I had the honor of coaching those games.

In 2009, I headed to Brazil. As I said before, I already knew a little about the program.

As always, my first job is to position myself with the best information, such as:

- What players I have.
- What competitions I have scheduled.
- How much time I have to train that is compatible with the club calendar.
- What league matches I can attend.
- How to get to know and understand the thinking of the directors and the president.
- Were there possibilities to organize friendly matches in Brazil, outside, or on the way to American Championships or World Championships.

With all this information, I prepared a strategic plan and discussed it with the directors. I started a round of meetings with the coaches of the clubs (some of them I already knew) and the coaches of the national teams to discuss my plans.

The Brazilian handball elite is located south, around São Paulo. There were some good teams in the states of Santa Catarina and Paraná, as well as some in the northeast in Salvador, Aracaju, Maranhão, and Pernambuco, but due to the distance, they could not participate in the National League—which is a serious and competitive league with high-level teams which had structures that allowed the players to play professionally or semi-professionally.

The Men's National Team had good players, and once again I was surprised by the tactical quality and coordination Jordi Ribera implemented between them.

O Pais Maravilloso

The Women's National Team at the international level was more competitive, which in the Americas put them above the other national teams. There was a lot of institutional support, hard work from both the club and national coaches—including Juan Oliver who led the team for a while. There were also some players playing in Europe, which on one hand was very positive, but on the other hand it always created problems when combining schedules for the national team and the European Leagues. We will come back to this when we talk about the activities carried out during my leadership. The Men's Team at the international level was less competitive. Some players played in Europe, although less than the women.

The two junior teams (male and female) had some promising players. With all this information, I made the decision of who would be my direct assistants for the national team. We had a fairly solid and concrete understanding regarding the reality of the Brazilian handball team that we had to work with in the next three years.

There was a high level of performance from the adults and juniors. Primarily in the clubs, but I think it was necessary to be organized with a strong base for development of players to guarantee continuity as veteran players retired.

Jordi Ribera had already worked on this issue in Blumenau with a school faculty that combined the ages of cadets and children.

We presented two plans. One would be to increase the number of training camps for junior male and female players by adding players who demonstrated potential and try to improve the make-up of the national teams. Most of these actions were carried out in Praia Grande.

The second plan was very similar to the Base and Talent Detection Program that we used in Spain because so many successes were achieved in the thirty or forty years it had been applied.

We separated the children and cadet groups and would work with players selected according to previous assessments. Many training camps were held with adults and juniors (male and female) in Praia Grande, but the Base Program did not go as planned.

On the Women's National Team some young players were added, and the quantity and quality of training in Praia Grande was increased, complementing the work in the clubs.

As mentioned before, the players who played on the European teams had trouble with the dual scheduling, especially the team from Hypo Bank in Vienna,

Austria. To solve that, the president and I met in Vienna with the board of Hypo Bank to negotiate the schedule with the national team.

Coaching Always A Pleasure

Not only did things work better for the players, but later an additional four team members joined Hypo Bank. Strategically, preparations were organized in Vienna in which those players did not have to travel.

The women's team was a good team, and under the direction of Morten Soubak, their Danish coach, dominated American handball going on to earn fifth in the 2011 World Cup in Brazil and becoming Champions of the World in 2013, in Serbia.

The Men's Team had more difficulty in terms of results because the opponents had improved a lot. During the time I worked in Brazil, the first three places in the matches in the Pan American Championships were always highly contested. However, thanks to Argentina's "golden" generation, it was slightly superior. Chile and Uruguay improved a lot, along with Cuba and Greenland who almost always shared the successes.

The team was tactically sound, but we needed to incorporate young players in positions to accompany the veterans whose experience was important. Yet, some of the older players held us back, diminishing the danger of our attack, especially our defense.

I started working a few months before the 2009 World Cup in Croatia where I attended as an observer. I lived with the team, but they already had their coach (Washington Nunes). It was very useful to see them compete.

I must say that despite the financial difficulties that existed in the Federation when the sponsorship of Petrobras failed, they were always able to provide sufficient financial support to all the programs and activities we proposed. We had a program of training and competition activities, but for a long time I realized the rivalry between South American teams and the Brazilian and Argentinian teams were something out of the ordinary. The matches caused anxiety and stress and the team's performances did not equate to the level of the other teams' efforts. In the time I worked with them, we were only able to beat Argentina in the South American Games in Medellín, Colombia.

This was another reason why the entry of young players was very important. Such as the left side, Tiagus; the right winger, Fabio; the pivot, Vinicius, and the left winger, Gil—a great beach handball player who was very useful the short time he was with us, especially on defense.

This combination of players constituted a good team that could play very well, suffer a slump, or show an inability to control their nervousness and anxiety at times, which produced the irregularity that characterized us.

Brazil was perhaps the country where I found myself most frustrated and unhappy with my job as a coach. We got the Federation to give us everything we needed to prepare. We trained well, we competed well in preparation matches outside of and inside Brazil, but we were not able to win the games. And yet, it was very important to win in the American competitions. Specifically, the Pan American Championships qualifying for London 2012.

During the months before the competition, we trained, and we had managed to get some teams to come to Brazil to help us prepare. We played two games against Tunisia, and we won; two against Denmark, we won one and lost the other, and two against Cuba which we won. The previous year we played Italy, England, and Iceland.

In the finals of the tournament, we played against Argentina and we were winning by six goals in the first half. Yet, we lost after multiple errors in the second half.

Losing that game was a hard blow for me as a coach. I saw no reason to play that way, and I began to question if I really had something else to contribute or if I should let someone else take command for the 2016 Olympiad in Rio de Janeiro.

Apart from all this, multiple clinics and conferences were held throughout the country with two clear objectives: dissemination of ideas and search for young players. On this highlight, an idea the Brazilian Federation had surprised me, because I never saw it in other Federations. Every year the Federation organized a symposium, inviting all handball teachers from all the universities that have a program of our sport in their curriculum. This together with the fact that handball is included in the Physical Education programs in the schools guaranteed continuity. The sharing of ideas and information from the top of the sport to the base was beneficial.

One big accomplishment I am very pleased to have played a role in from the beginning was to create a training center. After meetings and discussions with the competent authorities of the City of San Bernardo, the board of the Federation decided to create an Olympic Handball Training Center on the grounds of a former sports club of the Volkswagen factory in that city. This included training and game pavilions, spaces for gyms, swimming pools, medicine, and rehabilitation clinics, as well as research laboratories, center management offices, rooms to teach courses, and finally dormitories, and dining rooms. It was inaugurated sometime after I left. I hope it is working at full capacity.

The organization of the Women's World Cup in 2011, coincided with the beginning of the financial crisis in Brazil, which caused the termination of many sponsorship contracts.

In the case of handball, it was Petrobras, which together with the withdrawal of the commitment previously made by the State of Santa Catarina very shortly before the start of the World Cup, forced it to be played in São Paulo. Thus, further increasing the burden of expenses the Federation would have to assume.

These months of stress in the Federation, and that feeling that my time as coach of the national team could have come to an end, led to my decision not to renew at the end of my contract. So, after that final against Argentina, I spoke with President Manoel Luis Oliveira, despite the discomfort we both had—in my case, for not having been able to give him a better result that would have facilitated his work. Everything ended with a meeting with Manoel Luis, the players, and me, in which I announced to the players I was not continuing at the end of my contract as National Coach.

During the last months and the previous chain of events, my wife and I had come to the conclusion that maybe it was time for us to end this wandering life. We planned our departure from Brazil and were clear that our life should be focused on living in the United States where our children and grandchildren were settled, specifically in Virginia near Washington, DC.

We still had our house in Colorado Springs that had been rented all this time since 1987 when we left for Spain.

The plan was to go to Colorado Springs and recover the house, then Linda would look for work as a teacher, I would retire, and I would be the cook and head of the house. It was the year 2012. I was sixty-five years old, and my body was starting to tell me something, so we decided to communicate that to our children.

Nonetheless, as it happened all my life, handball had a new surprise waiting for us.

In December 2011, we were in the stands watching one of the matches of the World Cup in Brazil. I met Miguel Roca, and, in the conversation, it was revealed that when I finished the work in Brazil, I would go to the USA to retire. Miguel informed me there was a new president of the American Federation. At the time, I did not know the new president because he had recently assumed the post. After a while I was introduced to President Jeff Uthz and Julio Sainz. Later I found out Julio Sainz was a coach from Los Angeles who accompanied Jeff and helped him with the translations.

We sat down to talk, and in the conversation, Jeff asked if I could help them since they were looking for a coach for the Men's Team. I explained my plans to go to the USA, and I implied I might be interested, but I needed to talk about it with my wife. They liked the idea, and we met the next day at his hotel. Jeff explained the plans of the Federation and I liked what he said. By the end of the meeting, I was one of the candidates for the position of USA Men's Coach. We exchanged contacts and agreed that he would call me if we would proceed with those arrangements. A week after the championships, he called to tell me that in a few days they had a meeting in Salt Lake City, Utah. It would be a brainstorming session with all the levels of the Federation to decide what should be done in the future and that they wanted me to attend the meeting. I was delighted to go.

A few days later, I flew from Santos, Brazil to Salt Lake City, USA for two days to discuss the plans of the Federation. It also gave me the opportunity to meet some new people. It ended up being a total of five days because the ticket they sent me was cheaper to stay longer.

After my visit to Utah and a few appropriate meetings, when I returned to Brazil, I informed my family I would be the future coach of the Men's Team of USA as soon as I finished my commitments in Brazil.

I made sure to notify Manoel Luis, so that he knew not to count on me at the end of the contract. There was little time left for the Pan American Championship—the famous final with Argentina in which I convinced myself I did not have much more to offer the team. Though we prepared for the match with Argentina, we were not able to win.

Before entering the meeting in which we would inform the players, Manoel Luis offered that I continue for a short time as coach and then join the organization of the Rio 2016 Olympic Games. I rejected the offer.

Manoel Luis is one of the people I have dealt with the most internationally and whose trustworthy friendship I am most proud of. These were not easy times for the Brazilian Federation, but once again Manoel Luis rose to the occasion.

Moves, packages, furniture, selling belongings—the usual things we go through—and at the end of the tunnel, Linda and I safely arrived in Colorado Springs. I started my position in the USA Handball Federation, and we settled back in our beloved house.

The situation in the Federation was different from what I knew. There were new people, many legal and political problems, a long list of changes of presidents and directors, and a list that goes on.

All this surrounded of course by the constant sword of Damocles. There was no money, so the ideas and promises contributed by each of the new candidates became nothing when they reached the presidency. Some still recited the same speech that had been made twenty-five years ago.

The penultimate of these cases was a Utah businessman who, when he left, his vice president Jeff Uhtz took the reins and promoted the meeting in Salt Lake City with some influence in USA Handball, but nothing really changed.

The representatives of the Olympic Committee told everyone they first had to establish and consolidate the structure around the Federation office in Colorado

Springs and promote the organization. Despite the many years some of the key people dedicated to propagate, organize, and fight for the development of handball, not much was accomplished. Many of these leaders should have waited or stepped aside to make way for the new generations.

One key discussion and topic of confrontation between the "patriarchs" of each side of the primary debate:

1. Forget the national teams and dedicate yourself only to youth development.
2. Boost the national teams, win medals, and you will draw in the youth.

In the USA, handball is not part of the Physical Education curriculum in schools.

In the universities it is not included in what is called varsity sports—the sports we all know, basketball, American football, baseball, etc. Varsity sports have scholarships, competitions, and four-year programs.

We have what are called clubs. That is to say, a group of students who know handball (European immigrants, those who were attracted after watching televised Olympic Games), who meet one or two times a week, and "practice" by playing for a while and having a beer afterwards. Once a year, there is a College National Championship that occurred during the weekend (Saturday and Sunday), and the clubs of several universities would travel to that site and play about five or six games in two days.

At the same time, some universities in different parts of the country had good programs. They trained a little more and took the competition more seriously.

The other important groups in the development of handball are the clubs: groups of people who get together, each pay the rent of the gym where they play and then they compete in the National Club Championship.

These clubs are distributed in various parts of the country (New York, Chicago, Los Angeles, Colorado, etc.). Most are a make-up of European immigrants who have already played in Europe or know handball. The pity is that the average age will be around forty.

That said, once again there are some clubs that work seriously within their means and have contributed many players to the national team, and their coaches are part of the history of American handball.

You can already imagine that in all this time and explanation there is no money, and the players and coaches have to bear their expenses.

The Federation and the Olympic Committee are private entities which do not receive any subsidy. They have to raise money from private donors, and in the USA, there is no Ministry of Sports or higher sports council. Everything has to be raised privately.

Now, in each Olympic cycle, and due to the fact that handball is an Olympic sport, you enter some circles and belong to some organizations such as the Olympic Committee, Olympic Games organization committees, and the IHF. These organizations get money and can allow the Federation to create programs and participate in international competitions (Pan American, Olympics, World Championships), and that's where the coaches of the national teams and those who work in the offices of the Federation come in. We are the only ones who get paid.

Returning to the meeting in Utah, the argument to focus on youth development and wait thirty years was not favored, so it was decided to continue with both priorities as always. Promote handball as much as possible in schools, colleges, and clubs, and try to get enough money to have a minimum program that allowed you to have the national teams train and compete at the Pan American level and qualify for World Championships and Olympics.

I started working in the summer of 2012, once I settled in Colorado Springs. My job was to visit the areas where we had some activity or new areas where we could organize clinics and events to promote handball.

Every two or three months we held tryouts, an activity or training session for the evaluation of players for future opportunities to concentrate on training and competitions which we could organize. All this constituted what we called regional work. Also, during 2012 and 2013, we held many meetings and designed a strategic plan to present our clubs and players with the idea of evaluating and selecting a group of players who were willing to move to a new location to train daily, while gaining the chance to be a part of the World Championships and

Olympics later. This was what we did in the past—July 1981 to July 1984 in Los Angeles, and 1994 to 1996 in Atlanta.

Several options were considered as to where this work should be done. One of the ways I looked for players was to contact coaches of basketball, American soccer, baseball, and volleyball and ask them if they knew athletes with certain qualities among their players or someone who had recently graduated.

Some of the players I worked with from 1979 to 1984 and later, were or had been coaches in universities in basketball, volleyball, etc. One of them specifically, Reita Clanton, played basketball, volleyball, and softball for Auburn University in Alabama.

Later she worked as a basketball coach and had been an Assistant Coach in handball at the Atlanta Olympiad. I called her and asked about players with characteristics that I mentioned before. I explained that we were trying to create another program similar to the one for LA '84 and Atlanta '96.

Reita told me to give her a couple of days and she would tell me something. The next day she called me and told me the Department of Kinesiology of the university was very interested in promoting and helping with the Residency Program we wanted to set up, and to propose a meeting the next week between Auburn University and the USA Federation.

A week later, I, the vice president, and manager in charge of the national teams in the Federation attended a meeting, listened to proposals, and explained our plans. The offer to work with Auburn was very clear. It was great for us and was approved without problem at the next Federation meeting.

BASIC CONDITIONS

Auburn University through its Department of Kinesiology would host our program and provide:

1. Training and a game facility (a gym with capacity for 14,000 spectators).
2. Medical services and physiotherapy.
3. Testing of the Women's and Men's Teams (physiology, biomechanics).
4. In-state tuition for any players wishing to attend classes, even if they were from another state. (A student from outside Alabama paid about $25,000 per year. One from Alabama paid $9,000).

Auburn Alabama

Our plan was to train every day in the evening with at least three full practices per week. Players could have access to the facilities for extra conditioning or go to school/work during the day.

It took a couple of months to assemble all this, but in 2014, the Residency Program of the national handball teams was created in Auburn, Alabama. Therefore, the García Cuesta family sold their house in Colorado Springs and bought a house in Opelika next to Auburn, Alabama). I started working with the Men's Team, while the Women's Team worked with their coach Christian Latulippe.

Panam Championship

The work and effort of players, directors, teachers, coaches, doctors, and physiotherapists eventually gained recognition from the USA Olympic Committee, and Auburn was declared an Olympic Handball Center.

A year and a half later, the International Handball Federation (IHF) offered to create in Auburn, the third IHF academy in the world (at that time there were only two in China). The intervention of IHF president Dr. Hassan Moustafa was fundamental and contributed greatly to the prestige and support for our program.

The program continued with its pros and cons, great possibilities, and also some challenges. We will talk about all this in a later chapter.

Handball Olympic Training Center

In September 2017, Linda, my wife, died suddenly. Then in 2018, I retired, and I resigned from my obligations in the USA Federation. Thirty-two years of coaching the national teams—thirty-eight years if we add two plus one with Teka (club in Santander and three more as RFEBM Technical Director).

If we continue adding my eight years as a "professional" player, and the four years as a physical trainer of football, it would be about fifty years dedicated to and living with the sport.

So far this has been my story and how it unfolded. In the following chapters we will develop how we worked and what the final results were.

Javier García Cuesta

CHANGES IN INTERNATIONAL HANDBALL CONDITIONED MY EVOLUTION AS A COACH

My time as an elite handball player (1967–1976) undoubtedly had an important influence on my development as a coach, especially in my early years. All the jobs and lessons I received from my coaches, plus four years of teaching at the INEF in Madrid, in addition to learning under the orders and direction of two masters of handball teaching Domingo Bárcenas and Juan de Dios Román (both rest in peace) influenced me greatly.

My generation was among the first to make the qualitative leap in terms of amount of work. Training morning and afternoon still did not have the acceptance it has today. We were the generation who said, *"You can't drink water."* Our primary strategy was to defend and counterattack. Yes, I know this is still used today, but the circumstances were very different years ago. We knew if that did not work, we would be challenged to win, because in the organized attack we had serious problems. But this strategy did work, thanks to the quality of our shooters (Juan Morera, Sagarribay, Tono Andreu); the intelligence and ability of our pivots (Quico Balcells, José Taure); the "whatever was necessary" of Fernando de Andrés, plus the elegance and speed of Pitiu Rochel. And we cannot forget the security we had—Perramón, who would block goals in our glorious defense. The Medina brothers, Jesús Gurrero, Juan Igartua, Alfredo Alonso, dozens of great players (Villamarín, Santos Labaca).

In our work, there were always veteran and younger players mixed in the team and each had their own idiosyncrasies. Coaches also had their own teaching methods to which the players were subjected, and as players, we all learned the ideas and beliefs of our coaches. The current reality, the past, and the future are very mixed, but each one always improves the previous one because the new players start from what the old ones did after years of improving what the previous players lacked.

The activities of the national team increased considerably while the promotion of handball increased both at the club and national team levels. Television began to broadcast matches. Every year we had some activity of the national team, and I was lucky enough to participate in the 1974 World Championship (East Germany) and the Munich 1972 Olympiad.

Munich '72

I will try to summarize all I learned from the training, matches, and championships and explain how we played, and how handball was back then. And from there I'll add concepts, ideas, and changes leading up to how handball is today and something about current players.

I learned many different ways, including from a few joint trainings I've had in Romania. The Romanians at that time were World Champions, so it was a great help for us to train with them and play against them.

ATTACK

We imitated their game. Move the ball to put the defenders in place, and from there it was a game of crosses and screens; single or double; (center-pivot) for the shooter on duty to score. (Gruia, Birtolon, Stîngă, Zaharia).

This type of game had a problem because we did not have the shooters Romania had. Neither I nor the center, Gaţu were as capable. When we lost the ability to play vertically, we became a team that "played AMONG OURSELVES" making the tactical combinations, but we didn't play "AGAINST THE DEFENDERS"— opponents. Hence the importance of the counterattack in our offensive game.

DEFENSE

Fundamentally, we played 6–0 with a lot of shifting and defensive triangles (direct opponent out, the two defenders immediate to him on the right and left helped the blocking in 6 m).

If we could not stop their shooters, we went to 5:1 favoring the side of the best shooter or the organizer and the other five in the zone. We knew the 3-2-1 defense of the 1972 Munich Olympiad, and the 1970 World Cup Qualifier we played against Yugoslavia. Years later we improved the details when Cicanovic coached us at Atlético.

The next turning point in terms of knowledge and mastery was the vertical game of Poland in the 1974 World Cup, directed by its coach Prof. Janos Cerwinski. Great team, great players individually, but also "PLAYING AGAINST THE DEFENDERS" and not "AMONG THEM".

The principle was simple: Direct and vertical attack to the spaces between defenders and great quality 1:1. I finish if I can. If I do not, I pass to the immediate or distant partner to finish. That is, the attack is divided into smaller groups (from 6:6 of the Romanians to 2:2 of the Poles), and the principle of continuity is created if I cannot finish my attack.

Because of these different playing styles, we had a need for quick adaptation of the attack and Prof. Bárcenas came to us with the idea to vary our angles of attack (curvilinear, oblique, right left, left right). The idea was to surprise the defender with different approaches and thus facilitate the success of the 1:1 confrontation.

This takes time for the players—especially those who were not INEF students—to adapt to this way of playing, which makes me return to the importance of being aware of the different generations and mentalities found on our team. Meanwhile there were some memorable situations like those that occurred in the Mediterranean Games in Algeria.

All this might seem anecdotal, but it served as the basis after much training, teaching, and experimentation by coaches and players regarding the concept of matching defenses that came later and brought us so many successes and achievements.

Some characteristics of the great teams of that era:

ROMANIA:
- 6:6 circulation of the ball and players to facilitate the launch of your specialist.

POLAND:
- Vertical play.
- Physical quality – technique of Yugoslavia and its group game (usually 3 players)

SOVIET UNION (The best of all at that time in my opinion):
- Goal scorer on the left side.
- Pivot large static blocks in 6 m.
- Right side without left-handed.
- Central director but also dangerous.
- Fast and very good wingers; they see the other four play in the organized attack and run like fallow deer in the counterattack.
- Goalkeeper not very mobile but huge.

NORDIC TEAMS:

- Great passing technique.
- Closed tactics with several final solutions.

THE TWO GERMANYS:

- With complete players, although perhaps more mechanized.
- Strong personalities; various experts in the competition perhaps due to the experience of the Bundesliga.

Little by little we joined this list as did countries such as France and Portugal. Later the countries of North Africa, Algeria, Egypt, and Tunisia, sporadically, competitors from Korea as well.

Everything described so far in this section, plus the studies and the two years of handball mastery at the INEF, together with the National Course of Coaches was part of my experience and connection to handball strategy. My way of seeing the sport would help me to successfully solve the difficulties and problems that would surely arise later in my coaching career.

Everything pointed in that direction, I would play two or three more years, I would continue to absorb more knowledge and experiences until finally retiring and becoming a handball coach.

Then, as I explained earlier, the opportunity arose to become a physical trainer of Atlético Madrileño (subsidiary and second professional team of the club), and later of the first professional team, Club Atlético Madrid of the First Division of Football.

At the end of the 1975–1976 season, I retired from handball and continued for three more years, only working in football. It was a moment of total change in my professional life. I completely detached myself from handball and lost that ongoing source of knowledge and experience I had while being an elite player and Physical Education student.

I dedicated myself completely to soccer, and for this I used all possible tools to increase my knowledge of the game. In two years, I did the Youth Coach Course at the Madrid Federation. The following year, the Regional Course and I also returned again to INEF to obtain a master's degree in soccer.

I want to recognize someone who was very important in my athletic career and one of my great friends, Victor Varela. He and I played handball together at school and at the Algodonera de Gijón. When I went home during Christmas or summer or whatever break we were on, Victor and I always saw each other. We trained with the teams of Gijón (Sporting and Grupo Covadonga), and we played ping-pong, needing a court nearly as big as a tennis court.

In a word, he was my confidant, and I always kept in mind many things he told me. The first time I went to Gijón, he was one of the first to inform me about football, since he played goalkeeper for a regional team.

My knowledge of soccer was limited to having played as a child in the neighborhood. Well, when I arrived in Gijón I met him on the beach of Estaño. Victor taught me football for more than two hours while his girlfriend sunbathed on the beach. There were also two things he and I did that I'm sure influenced me to become a professional coach.

When we were still young, the Heart of Mary School had a sector phase in A Coruña. Roncero, our coach, could not go so Victor and I enjoyed stepping in for the team.

The second year of our "studies" at the University of Oviedo, Victor and I played at the club Algodonera de Gijón. At the same time, we covered the news where we published weekly the Chronicle of the Match in the newspaper El Comercio and signed as CUVA.

Sorry for this departure from the subject, but it was important for two reasons:

1. I wanted to thank and mention my friend, Victor Varel.
2. I wanted to emphasize that for four years I completely forgot about handball.

I could count on one hand the number of matches I attended during that time. Since I was not playing or studying the sport, I lost that source of information and knowledge.

In August 1979, I was at the Olympic Training Center in Squaw Valley, California as coach of the U.S. Women's National Handball Team. This was when I began my journey of trying to recover the knowledge I lost. It used to be easy to understand, but by then the knowledge was long gone and not so easy. Adding to the pressure to relearn the sport, I was tasked with teaching it to players whose experience was very limited and, in some cases, zero.

The six months I worked with the Women's Team came in handy. I was lucky. Before me the girls had a coach who created techniques and taught the tactic of vertical attack, which facilitated a lot when I arrived with my "Spanish ideas" of variety, imagination, and surprise.

Once I returned from Europe, the two national teams (men's and women's) trained for several weeks at the Olympic Center in Colorado Springs. This gave me the opportunity to not only get to know the players on a personal level, but it also gave me the opportunity to study their level of performance.

In the end, despite the promises of the Olympic Committee Directors, the USA boycotted the Moscow 1980 Olympic Games.

During this time, I worked as Technical Director of the Federation, traveled to organize clinics, visited clubs, and attended regional and national competitions. By the way, in one of these jobs helping and contacting clubs, I went to do some training with Texas A&M University. We finished the job going to Mexico to a tournament in which I ended up playing for what would be my last games as a player.

Texas A&M

The anecdotal culmination of this experience was to meet Gruia, the legendary scorer from Romania who worked for the Mexican Olympic Committee, and whom I had the opportunity to introduce to the team. It was very nice, and years later we would see each other again across several American competitions.

In March 1980, when the boycott was confirmed, the work of the national teams ended. From the trip to Europe (Romania and Bulgaria) with the girls in August 1979 until July 1981, when we started the program to prepare for LA '84, with daily training and periodic trips to Europe, I had very little contact with the elite handball team. That year and a half can be added to the other three (1976–1979), which makes four and a half, almost five years in which I was mostly away from handball.

Logically I had to catch up as soon as possible through experience and studies. The preparation, direction, and evaluation of matches would come with time.

Several things helped in relearning the game:

1. I had the opportunity to speak with opposing coaches. The official dinners after the games were the "advantages" of traveling together with the physiotherapist. Being the only officer of our entourage forced me to be the coach, but also the one who prepared the entire itinerary from hotels to meals and more. In most cases, I was also the one who gave the speeches of thanks and protocol, and essentially placed me in privileged places which allowed me to network with officials. Very special conversations were held with B. Procrayac, A. Yestuchenco, Mosai, B. Johansson, P. Otto Furuseth, Vlado Stenzel, J. Cerwinski, D. Constantini, and many more.

    Of course, it is also mandatory to mention Domingo Bárcenas and Juan de Dios Román, who meant so much in my learning. To those who followed, Emilio Alonso, Juan Antón, Sergio Petit, Pep Villa, and of course José Antonio Roncero. And later Manuel Laguna, Luis Carlos Torrescusa, Paco Sánchez, Jordi Álvaro, and Cruz María Ibero who were also important.

2. I also took advantage of the facilities and services of the physiology laboratory of the Colorado Springs Training Center and an agreement with the University of Massachusetts. We did some studies of effort assessment in handball to compare work in games and training sessions.

    Then we did a project during competition, specifically the Women's World Championship in Hungary in 1982, and the Men's

Championship in the Netherlands in 1983. Games were filmed with high-speed cameras, tracking the players with a dot, and the camera recorded their every move.

We measured distance traveled during the game, speed at which they moved, and the percentage of times they moved at different speeds.

The work of comparison between the laboratory data and the data collected during the training gave us the degree of minimum intensity and maximum cardiac pulsation of the critical training zone, as well as aerobic–anaerobic threshold, that is, to what percentage of the maximum aerobic capacity the player has. The player goes from working aerobically to anaerobically. It was an exhilarating and productive time in my career.

Italy 1987

3. In 1987, we did work with the Men's National Team in collaboration with the University of North Carolina—led by John Silva, professor of sport psychology—studying the players and the team, as well as my work as coach of the team. It was carried out in three phases:

    i. We did a five-day training camp at the university. John Silva and his assistants interviewed the players individually and in groups. They generated individual chips and observed the training.

   ii. He traveled with us to Italy where we played the 1987 World Championship, and for a week he observed the pre-training and training sessions.

   iii. He and I talked informally, but also every morning we went for a run together and discussed all the situations regarding the players. I also evaluated my performance during training and matches. The rest of the day he would interview and talk to the players. We would end the day meeting him and the rest of the staff, sometimes with players around the campfire.

At the end of the seven days in Italy, he had to leave, and we were still in competition. Then I went to Chapel Hill, North Carolina, and we discussed the results and the report I generated for the Federation. I was very happy with this experience. There was supposed to be a fourth phase of work, but unfortunately because of different agendas and scarcity of money, it ended there.

Nonetheless, I left with a great friendship that united me and my family with Professor Silva. The passion for our sport created one of the best university handball programs in the country.

When we competed in Europe after my five-year hiatus from handball, it forced me to retrain myself. The first of the evolutions I found were the "arm feints" toward strong points and weak points.

We watched and studied these movements and then I spent time in the hotel room repeating the movements to the right and left until I was able to master them acceptably. Several days later I taught my players how to make the arm feint.

I will now list some concepts or ideas that emerged and contributed to the development and evolution of handball and to which coaches had to adapt by introducing them into our attack systems, as well as in defenses to stop them.

ATTACK

1. The attacker needs to be closer to the defender. He seeks, with the help of his arms and torso, to use the space just behind the defender. As with any feint, the legs are very important in braking and

changing direction. The novelty goes through the arm when the ball passes over the head of the defender and the other hand is placed on the hip of the defender and makes it difficult for him to adjust. As always, it is easy to master this move after a while. Where was the one who invented this when I was playing?

2. Players need to improve their jumping, which gives them more time to decide the location of a shot or pass (threads, base lines, different steps, different throwing forces, etc.).

3. Appearance of bigger players which produced more physical contact. Also, a lot of slowness—especially in bringing the ball down the court by the second wave (first line and large pivots), but there was almost always a direct counterattack. This slowness caused the beginning of discussions in congresses at IHF on the need to accelerate the movement of the ball up the court. At this time Sweden was dominating its counterattack with wings on the ends and the pivot, and later some tactical combination of the second wave (first lines, usually large crosses).

    The continuation of all this led to many discussions to change rules such as enforcing when throwing out at midcourt after a goal. It is not necessary to wait for the entire opposing team to pass the midcourt. This was a big change for handball. The coaches had to rethink the methods and strategies of training. At the beginning it was commented that perhaps we would look more for the smallest and quickest players instead of the ones who were stronger, but slower and unable to withstand that rhythm of play. After a while, the training improved, and the big players ran and endured the new and fast paced plays.

4. Finally, another critical point in the development of modern handball was the appearance with total confirmation in the World Cup in Portugal 2003, of Croatia and the extraordinary contribution of its center Balić becoming the best player in the world during that era. A total innovator by reversing the concepts established until then.

    We moved the ball and players in certain tactical combinations so certain players found several possibilities of completion. Balić instead did the opposite and put everyone in their place. He took the ball, and directly attacked his opponent with such tenacity that it was very difficult to stop a 1:1. Most of the time it required at least another defender to help. Against these two defenders, he attempted to score, which he often did, or if it was not possible, he made the decision to pass to the best placed player in all the angles and planes of the game. He was a 360-degree player. That is, he could pass to the right side, left side, deep forward to the pivot, or behind to one of the back-court players who started a circulation in crossing behind him.

These simple ideas are the culmination, refinement, and simple explanation of strategies from generations of players and coaches that we have all heard for years. We often had good organization, and things would go well. When nothing went as we wanted, in that case, our game could be disorganized and chaotic.

For all these years of work, training, and imitation of the game like the Yugoslavian "improvisation," we eventually learned that improvisation came with training and repetition. The variety and quality of the Russian central defenders, the Swedish teams with their closed tactics, but several finishing actions. And why not the varied and brilliant game of Spain that was evolving from the Romanian game to the "curvilinear trajectories." This resulted in the succession of generations of players who were debugging and improving each other until they reached success.

The funny thing about all this is, despite the connection between the different generations, each one has its own characteristics. We think that we are already at the highest possible level, but you realize you have played at your highest capacity for ten years, and neither I nor any coach presented ourselves in front of a goalkeeper from the end and threw a "Rosca." One of the most important principles of handball is that no matter how good you are, you can always become better.

I also want to note the improvement of the pivot game. For instance, increased receptions with one-hand while the other created space from the defender. Another innovation was the quality of the passes to the pivot inside the area of 6 m which forced them to jump from outside the area, receive the ball in the air, and finish with the defender on top trying to deflect the ball to prevent the shot.

This confrontation of the pivot with defenders in a very small space and the connection with the rest of the teammates contributed greatly to the positive evolution handball has experienced. A clear example is the game and skills of Uríos, the pivot for Spain.

When the rule of the substitution of the goalkeeper for another court player was modified, it stated, "It does not have to be the same player who replaces the goalkeeper if he has to return to the goal."

I am not in favor of using this rule because I think the risk of losing the ball and the other team scoring is greater, but it is another tool to use if you think it is necessary.

DEFENSE

In my time we usually defended 6–0 with a lot of shifting, using defensive triangles to create the maximum possible block in front of the ball. Sometimes we added a little variety by pressing and not allowing the wingers to receive the ball. This did not allow support and extreme-lateral movements which forced teams to play the game toward the center, thus reducing the width of the attack and directing it toward our central defensive block. We knew the strategies and missions of the defenders in 5–1 and 3–2–1.

We used 5–1 mixed if we could not stop the back-court shooters outside the 9 m with our zone defense, or if we had to interfere in the tactical organization of the opponents by marking the opposing center individually.

From 1979/1980, I resumed my career as a handball coach in the USA, and especially from 1981/1982 when we traveled and competed in Europe, I saw and learned the hard way with the following trends.

1. The 6–0 defense of Russia. Very big players a few steps away
   from the 6 m, blocking shots, and sometimes the pressure to
   attack wings as was mentioned previously. A lot of predisposition
   of the wingers to counterattack and fast break.

2. The Nordic 6–0 defense (Sweden, Denmark, Germany). Exit 9 m from the third defender and a lot of collaboration with the goalkeeper. Very effective defense in the block (with the center four) against shots from outside. Also excellent, improvement and generational succession of goalkeepers (C. Helgren, Matts Olsson T. Svensson). The counterattack from the wingers to the corner, and the coordination in crosses of the first line in the second wave was like a natural continuity of their defense. All this later gave them supremacy over the other teams for almost ten years.

3. Late '80s and mid-90s, Spain with Juan de Dios Román Seco as INEF professor and national team coach, introduced the 6-0, but open defense was more aggressive and with the defenders further out invading the attack zone. The basics position of the defenders was at 7-8 m but they would go out to 9-10 m and be able to return to 6-7 m. The second defender would leave early to attack the shooter. The pivot was marked between the two central defenders and the center defenders would also leave early to attack the center back.

As far as the 1:1 on the outside and if the winger splits to 2-4, we accompany him until we deliver him to the next defender, and we take out the first attacker (back-court). It was an innovative and effective defense and brought us a little closer to the Nordic countries who were not used to having defenders attacking them at 9 m. And at the same time there were no free spaces in 6 m to play with the pivots.

Here we find an exception in North Africa as Algeria, Egypt, Tunisia, and Morocco began to apply other principles and developed man-to-man defense.

Entering the zone and attacking at 8-11 m can be effective, retreating back to 6–8 m with the ball is on the opposite side.

You need a good pivot defender with large spaces, which is possible if you have a defender who uses his arms well to intercept passes to centers.

With any entry at 2:4, the defender accompanies him until he can hand him off by giving him to the center, and taking the next attacker. In the crosses, there is no change and 1:2 is played.

The biggest innovation with this defense is: it is played not only against the opponent, but also against the ball more clearly than in other more zone defenses.

This type of defense created a lot of controversy and a lot of interest. The concept of open defense occupied a lot of discussion time in clinics and symposiums–especially in Europe.

All this controversy and debate provoked some theoretical and practical work that improved the original idea of the Algerian team in the '80s.

Time went by and the evolution of the original idea occurred. Whenever I had to be the leader of a defensive clinic, I was approached with the following questions:

- Is it a man-to-man defense, or is it zone?
- Do they follow the opponent, or do they act against the pass line?
- How can opponents change with such large spaces?
- How do they mark the pivot with so much free space?
- Who stops a good 1:1 full-back or center-back with that space?
- What happens when someone unfolds without a ball?

All these issues I experienced toward the end of my career as a player, but while their defense was effective, Algeria still did not have enough attacking power to jeopardize the result of the match against a good European team.

Over time things changed; the open defenses were applied in other countries like Egypt who totally adopted the strategy.

The results were that the teams playing this type of defense improved and, in some cases, surpassed the Europeans.

As coach of Spain, I had enjoyed the good performances of the Spanish team in the World Championship in what was then known as Czechoslovakia 1990. They defended 6-0 open and deep in this tournament, as well as in the German Super Cup. They took third place in the World Cup in Sweden and the Goodwill Games in Seattle, USA.

In 1995, I became the coach of the Egyptian team where I signed a one-year contract. When we began work, I found the players were used to this defense and were confident in defending their opponent at 7-8 or 9 m. As a European coach, although I knew how it worked, I found it difficult to see my defenders so separated and so far from 6 m. Once the situation was analyzed and we incorporated my strategies, it started working. That first year was a constant "struggle" between the players going forward to interfere in the passing lines, intercepting passes, and the ability to score a goal with few passes. With me in charge, my goal was to guide and direct them towards at least 7 m.

That backward movement and then the constant going forward marked our defensive tactical play. On the individual level, we did bodybuilding work with weights trying to improve our strength in 1:1.

We also had a more conservative zone defense in the event that the open defense did not go well. That's how I ended my first contract year with Egypt leading up to the Atlanta Olympiad.

After, Atlanta I signed a second three-year contract that would last until the 1999 World Cup in Egypt.

As I referenced in the earlier section, the first two months of returning to work were marked by meetings, discussions, and decisions to ensure we were all going in the same direction, and to not allow politics, different agendas, or ideas to interfere with the progress of the team.

An intermediate agreement was reached by mixing all the ideas—some we knew would be difficult to execute. We had three years to do it and above all, we had to convince the players in training that these ideas were possible.

The general terms were as follows:
1. We would use a 3-3 defense.

    The second defensive line against the first attacking line sought to press them and throw them back to separate the two attacking lines. Moving away the ends of the sides, the center, and sides of the pivot, caused opponents to lose their connection.
2. It was a zone defense, so despite the distances, there was still help, although sometimes this was minimal.
    *   DIAGONAL: Ball on one side, advanced and second on the other side go down to help.

- CENTER: Ball in the center, the two seconds go down closing and helping.
- EXTERIOR: Exteriors and seconds are on the same line, both are back in 6 m, or both go up to press.

3. How far did we go? 11 m? 12 m? 15 m?

The most frequent topics that we talked about before we were asked in the clinics.

- How the ball was defended in the passing lines with the opponent less than 6 m away when approaching. Focus more on the opponent and less on the ball.
- How the pivot was marked by a specialist covering the lines of pass, foreseeing and deterring a lot of quality opportunities in large spaces with tactical intelligence.
- The back-court with space was marked by our second defenders.
- The splits without the ball. We had no choice but to accompany attackers until changing with the center and taking the pivot.

FINAL CONSIDERATIONS

Many coaches might think this open defense cannot be good and has too many weaknesses. I already commented on the difficulties for me personally, but over time and especially when you see your players move with quality, the approach and confidence they have in the strategy, the results and numbers you see at the end of the game can cause you to feel differently. My efforts appeared as though they were failing, along with traditions and habits, but as I gazed at the Great Pyramids, hope rose in me saying, "Here I can do something different." We can make this work.

In any case, we were aware of our weaknesses. Here I will identify strengths and weaknesses of our team.

WEAK POINTS

- Problems with the pivot as a finisher and as a collaborator with others
- Splits without the ball to finish or to create spaces for others
- Pass and go with the pivot
- Splits with or without the ball change

- The marking of the pivot and the player who unfolds
- Problems in the 2:2 especially with the pivot

Clearly, we could see there were more problems with the second line (wingers and pivots) than the first (central and lateral back-court players).

Special places with special people

Great times, unexpected ending never forgotten

STRENGTHS

- In most teams, the scorers are the front line—we were strong there.
- The construction of the game and of the team starts and is based on the first line—again, we were strong there.
- The other team was not used to playing against our defense and would apply solutions to which it was not accustomed.
- There was a possibility their pivot would score 5 or 6 more goals, but their first line would score 7, 8, or less.

When I was with the team during 1995 to 1999, there was a time when the teams had a lot of problems with our defense. A typical case for us was the Sweden World Championships. They had great teams—of course better than ours—but the many games we played were lost by only a few goals. At least we won more than one.

It was very difficult for them to play against our defense because it was difficult for them to execute their tactics because our players did not allow them to pass and move the ball as they would like to. Also, their first line did not get the distances and situations their tactical combinations normally provided.

In the end they beat us, not by their organized attack but by their defense and counterattack.

In addition to this 3–3 defense, we trained and prepared all the others also (6–0, 3-2-1, 5–1). We used them as it suited. Sometimes we alternated all of the varying defenses, varying two in the same attack. We started the defense with one system and when the opposing team attacked on that system, we changed to another.

The most spectacular example for us was the draw against Spain in the 1997 Kumamoto World Cup, where we precisely used this strategy.

As the evolution in both defense and attack continued, the frontline players were now fast and resistant. The attack toward the center was increasingly effective.

The idea of defending 5–1 to strengthen the center arose. Everyone suggested the work of Richardson in the French defense and the Russian advances. This became popular. Coaches of different teams started their new 5–1 that replaced their 6–0. The teams introduced specialists in that position and sought out solutions. Once again, Spain set the tone and instilled the ideas of anticipation to the attacker. This meant if you allowed him to receive in the distance that he wanted and, in the time, he wanted, you were closer to the goal, which was not ideal.

This concept of anticipation brings with it the concept of dissuasion, that is, anticipating and placing myself in the passing lines or threatening them to create doubt in the passer—"Can I pass or not?" It will force the receiver of the pass to vary his original idea of attack with the consequent delay and slowdown of the attack. That is already a defensive victory and from here comes the next pass (continuity). The next attacker will have to make the same decision and play against the deterrence of the next defender. Attackers try to get close while defenders avoid it, keeping the success rate low, and again passing the responsibility of making the right decision along to the next player.

Another idea arose: marking the pivot by two defenders, the alternation and variety of who goes out against the first line and who stays with the pivot, forcing the attacker to have one more doubt in the decision making. This occurrence is too much for some players and forces them to stay or end up in this difficult situation producing a faulty throw or giving up the completion by producing a pass making the defense successful. There are players who go out to the attacker with the ball when the partner stays with the attacking pivot. The attacker observes, and decides if he can shoot or should pass to the pivot. Just before the player returns to the passing line and intercepts, the attacker with the ball reacts to his movement causing him to shoot but not with full force.

This combination of work deterred lateral–lateral passes by the outside, players. The variety of tasks in the 2:2 markings as well as the variety of tasks and good tactical reading of the advanced 5–1, where we mark to the center and sometimes to one of the laterals is effective. We always tried to maintain the connection with the block of five standing in the lines of passing from side-to-side, deterring these passes. Much of the work from the defenders in the center slowed down the passes.

It took some time for the team to master and strengthen these ideas. Sometimes the point defender did not bother enough or the central block could not block the shots. Yet the insistence and good work of the coaches and players turned original ideas into something routine for Spain while it was very difficult for many other teams. The development and evolution of all this and the constant struggle between attack and defense helped us to evolve and improve. It all culminated with the magnificent defensive play of the Spanish team in the World Championship in Tunisia in 2005, where we achieved a victory both in defense and in the attack.

Faced with our deterrence and the anticipation of the defenders, we caused a slowdown and break of our opponents' rhythm. The attackers began to use simple crosses as preparation to approach the defenders. They obtained good distances and angles of shots from which they felt safe. If I had to say which country was best at attacking this way, I would say Yugoslavia.

Another weapon that had been established everywhere as normal and began in Spain already in the '80s was *the splits*. A 2–4 in all its variety, splitting of central–lateral–extreme with or without a ball from the same side of the pivot or on the opposite side.

There were many ways to position players and the ball which complicated the defensive work by having defenders face different situations and also different players. In the end, everything, or almost everything ended with a 2:2 attack that made defense even more difficult.

SUMMARY

ATTACK

- Dynamism and very high pace in the four phases of the game:
    i. Defense
    ii. Counterattack
    iii. Organized attack
    iv. Defensive return
- Initiation of the fast game after a goal is scored.
- Strategies against the change of the goalkeeper.
- Shorter attacks by passive play interpretation.
- Simple swaps or crosses prior to the decisive attack to acquire inertia.
- Much more play with the pivot in 2:2 and inside the area.
- Great variety and effectiveness from wings.
- Effective shots from 9–10 m is always welcome.

All of the above leads to more shots and more goals in games.

DEFENSE

- Increase and improvement of goalkeeper save percentages.
- Deterrent work of defenders to lessen initiative and slow down the pace of attack.
- A lot of use of 5–1 with a specialist at point against opponent and ball, combined with changing and shifting positions in the first line.
- Greater awareness on the defense when we change goalkeeper.
- Defense of the pivot by intercepting passes, and legally battling for control of space outside and inside 6 m includes the constant attempt to prevent or deny the pivot getting the ball.
- It is increasingly necessary to have good shot blockers in the center when the attack goes to one side or to the middle.

I end this section by saying, at present, elite handball is a good show, increased by much better television production (repetitions at different angles, slow motion, etc.). Let's all strive to maintain a steady line of improvement and protect the future of our sport.

FUNDAMENTAL PRINCIPLES

I was born into a family in which sports meant attending a football match, maybe the arrival of the Vuelta a España de Ciclismo, and maybe riding a bicycle—to which I did not have a model to imitate. I was a rather shy boy, and I also had a few kilos left over.

When I started classes at the Heart of Mary School, I trained with the youth team. The seriousness, presence, and personality of our coach impressed me a lot from the beginning, and I am sure he was one of the aspects that greatly influenced my subsequent decision to become a professional athlete. There was a lot of time spent imagining one day I could dedicate myself professionally to the sport. When I could finally dedicate myself to it, there were a series of concepts that influenced me very positively as a player. I was very clear that those concepts would also benefit me in coaching. I will try to describe them. There is not an order of importance from first to last, but each one was important depending on the moment and the circumstance.

1. **ATTITUDE** is one of the most important qualities we all have to have in sport.

    The player must arrive at the training predisposed and prepared for everything. Attentive and positively open to all the theoretical information they could receive, and self-prepared through individual and collective warm-ups to execute the physical activities that are proposed with attention, discipline, and generosity transmittable to the companions around him.

    The equation $V = (C + H) \times A$ proposed by Victor Küppers demonstrates very well what I am trying to explain. The value of a player is equal to the sum of knowledge plus skill multiplied by attitude.

    It was always very difficult for me to endure working with a player who did not have a good attitude.

    Both when I was a player and when I became a coach, I always liked training more than the game in terms of enjoyment. I am very aware the raison d'etre of sport is the competition. It is the reason we train every day. I value and always will value the amount of work done in training and its relationship with the game. The game is a reflection of training, "We play as we train." For me the player who does not share this philosophy will find it difficult to play on my team.

2. **THE PLAYERS ARE THE PROTAGONISTS.** They are the ones who are on the court, and the coaches are there to help them play to the maximum of their possibilities and to know their maximum. With our methods possibilities are higher.

    Here I want to highlight a concept I always felt throughout my career as a coach. You are not the coach when you sign the contract or when your appointment is announced, you are when you do something the players believe will help them achieve their individual goals.

We all have some example of this, but I have one I always remember very pleasantly.

In one of our trips to Europe during the '80s, the USA team was playing against a team from the German Second Bundesliga. We were losing after the first half by five. I remembered the previous months we had worked on varying the splits. It was one of the points we practiced in the matches during that trip.

At halftime we decided we were going to play 3–3 with two centers playing without a left winger. I went directly to tactical scheming so as not to waste time in the splits from the right side because the right side of our attack was the most efficient in the face of competition.

We played the whole second half with this scheme and in the end, we won by three goals. The joy and satisfied faces of the players was worth all the effort and training we dedicated to this strategy in the months leading up to the trip.

There are still some of those players who—in meetings and informal talks today (thirty years later)—use this anecdote as an example of our development as a team and the personal pride of having been in that situation.

Highest point of USA Handball Indianapolis 1987 Pan Am Champions Qualification for Seoul Olympics 198

3. **KEEP PLAYERS WELL INFORMED** in team talks, video sessions, in individual conversations, etc. We must make sure the message we want to pass on has been properly understood.

   Before training begins, I keep the team in line and informed of the work we are going to do during the session, and maybe sometimes connect it with the previous session—thus giving continuity to the work. During training you have to retain information and maintain communication with the players, but be careful of talking too much. When the players are executing the exercises and working at high intensity, it is difficult for them to hear you. The last thing they need is the continuous blabber of the coach. When it is time to give a specific instruction, a gesture or body expression, or if necessary to stop the exercise, pass the proper information and then continue.

   Regarding giving attention to the player who "already knows everything," who believes he has already figured it out. I have a few points to make:

   - It is always good to have on the court a player who is your continuation from the bench—with whom you can communicate in difficult situations, and who is an intelligent and experienced player. But remember, on the court the good player recognizes the situation that is presented to him and reacts instinctively, in most cases thanks to his tactical intelligence (combination of knowledge, perception, and reflex execution).
   - On the court if the player has to think, it will be too late.
   - The best learning is the one we do after believing we already know everything.
   - The veteran and experienced has to be humble and willing to learn.
   - You always have to keep a *distance* from the players. The coach must be in a position and have a relationship that allows him to be available. The player has to feel he can contact and consult with his coach. However, there

always has to be a separation that the two parties know and accept. When you lose distance, you lose control.

4. **DISCIPLINE.** This is a very important section. Discipline is absolutely necessary on a team. No matter how well everything goes, there will always come a time when something is going to happen; where rules will need to be applied that were already established based on the team's previous acceptance. Therefore, everyone knows in advance.

The following concepts are very important to keep in mind:
- "Discipline applied to others is not a punishment, it is to help, to improve, to correct, and to prevent. It is not to humiliate or take a posture of revenge." – John Wooden.
- If possible, it is advisable to have a code of conduct that specifies the situations that may arise and are clearly explained to the players. The code of conduct is analyzed, discussed, and perhaps some amendments are suggested and then presented to the coach to consider. When he agrees (the negotiation can be extended), it is formalized and becomes the "constitution" by which everyone is governed. On my teams I always have the following structure:
  - The captain is the spokesman of the team. The connection between the team and coach is chosen by the players.
  - The team will also have a senate committee of two or three players the coach chooses based on personality and leadership over their teammates.
- Both the captain and the members of the committee do not have any extra privileges. On the contrary, they have some extra obligations.
- The committee functions as a buffer in the first moments of a conflict, allowing me to talk to them and perceive the player's point of view. This allows for calm discussion to avoid any further damage to the team.
- It also helps me to act proactively before an event that will put us in a situation with the least stress. For example, "What do you

think if, when we encounter problems X, Y, Z, we react with these measures?" When the committee accepts, the information is passed to the players and becomes our standard of conduct.

- In all aspects of the coach's work, it is important to *stay consistent.* From the beginning, you have standards, and you stick to them. The whole group (players and staff) understand and buy in. The team knows where we stand on any issue.

Returning to the code of conduct. I would like to draw attention to two incompatible concepts which have to be considered. On the one hand, the code of conduct must integrate all possible infractions which could occur and accompany them with the consequent punishment. We have to intellectually elaborate on all aspects with a minimum of generality so any infraction, however strange it may be, can be considered as part of the code. And on the other hand, if we describe in the code thirty possible violations, surely one day there will be thirty-one not included. Therefore, we cannot apply it. It is better to leave a margin of ambiguity to be able to accommodate everything.

EXAMPLE

Among some of the problems I had in my years as a coach, I chose this as an example to show you how useful the captain structure can be.

At Christmas in the '80s, we trained for a week and went to play the World University Championship in France in January. In this activity the players paid out of their own pocket for the trip to France.

We played about six games. I had three goalkeepers and the third did not play in any game, which caused him to be very angry. This circumstance was discussed with the players and all of them were aware paying for the trip did not mean the security of playing.

At one point, we were on the bus to return to the hotel, and this particular individual accompanied by another player, entered the area where I was sitting in the bus. When he passed by, he took off my cap and told me, "F. . . YOU." Nothing further occurred until later.

We arrived at the hotel, I met with the captain and the committee, and I told them he was off the team and would not play the rest of the trip. I wanted to send him home right then. I didn't want to speak with him any further. My plan was to inform the Federation and if they authorized me to send him home alone, I would take him to the airport and be done. I told the captain, "I will make a report to the Federation. The situation is as it is, but if he comes to talk to me and apologizes, and I see the right attitude and purpose, I may decide to incorporate him back onto the team and the incident on my part is forgotten." It took a day and a half, but he eventually came, and we talked. Everything was normalized and the report I presented to the Federation did not cause any punishment.

With this example you can see the importance of the captain and the committee. The problem occurred, they talked and convinced him to apologize. I did not have to deal with the player thus avoiding the risk of further confrontation.

ONE of the most pleasant time as Coach Indianapolis 1987

Indianapolis 1987

5. **PUNCTUALITY.** Punctuality should be part of discipline, but for me it is not only that a person is late, it is the lack of respect for others who have arrived on time. I can understand one day someone is twenty minutes late, but it is not worth it for someone who always arrives five minutes late.

Punctuality implies predisposition, meaning if the training starts at 5:00, exactly at that time is when we start the work. If you need half an hour more, come at 4:30. At 5:00 the whistle blows, and work begins.

Trip To Europe Working Group

6. **OTHER CONCEPTS**
   - Keep your distance, always have a good presence.
   - Maintain and defend your line of work.
   - The clear difference between character and reputation is that character is what you are, what you radiate, what you impose. Reputation is what others think of you. What matters is character.
   - In your objectives and goals *aim higher*, you can always go down and adapt to the difficulties the work is presenting to you, and you have a margin of error that gives you room to adjust.
   - It's better to be naive, enthusiastic, and confident in your qualities than to be shy, not try, and then regret not doing it.

- Your plans and goals have to be realistic. Players are not stupid, and only if they fully accept your premises will these plans be possible.
- You can be very intelligent. You can know a lot, but the most important thing for a coach is to have common sense.

Working Help Always Friendship

I would like to finish this section referring to qualities a coach must have. I consider myself more a national team coach than a club coach. It could be due to the fact that for one reason or another I worked thirty-two years with national teams and only two-and-a-half years with Club Teka Santander. Nonetheless, I have always felt more identified with the immediacy and specificity of the work being focused on a certain competition. This was done through selection of the best players and training them to play tactically as a team in the short time we had playing every week for a whole year.

As coaches, regardless of whether we are with a club or a national team, our plans and work programs must take into account two things that may seem incompatible, but in reality, they are not and we as coaches must make the goals possible.

- We work to get maximum results as quickly as possible
- We must leave the team in a better situation than we found it

The first is easy. The success or failure of our work is marked by the results we have achieved as a team and future teams.

The second means the renewal of the team, adding new talent, improving the video analysis department, training more and better, and improving the facilities (gym, weight training room, physiology and biomechanics laboratory, etc.) will also aid in the success of the team.

MANAGEMENT AND LEADERSHIP OF THE WORKING GROUP (STAFF)

Given the complexity and amount of variables coaches have to handle today, it is very difficult for one person to manage all of them alone. It is increasingly necessary for specialists to be around to help the coach manage these variables.

Keep in mind the risk of having too many voices working around the team as the message will be diluted and fade. This causes confusion around each expert's area of expertise rather than helping to spread the main message of the coach.

The staff is a team in itself along with the coach. It is integrated as part of the bigger team formed together by the players and the coach.

- The staff must be competent and must demonstrate professionalism and organization in front of the players
- Those heads of specific team functions are experts; therefore, the coach must know how to delegate and let others take the reins when circumstances require it.
- Let's not forget we can also choose to be the "Base Elite" or the "Base of the Elite."
- The normal staff might include: coach, assistant coach, physiotherapist, video specialist, delegate. From here we can add depending on the financial capabilities: physical trainer, doctor, more assistant coaches, goalkeeper coach, psychologist, etc.

Side note: Sometimes the coach, perhaps an assistant and the delegate will have to assume all the functions including those of father and spiritual director!

Lastly, I want to finish with a suggestion I consider basic. It is the first and most important given, CONFIDENTIALITY. These people who work as a team with me will be in meetings, conversations, etc. where they will receive and know information that is always absolutely confidential and under no excuse can be disclosed. If that happens and this person divulges that information beyond the people who were in the meeting, immediately that person is off my team.

Of course, sometimes coaches do not have the authority to fire an employee of the club. In that case, perhaps the person can continue in the club in another position. If it is possible, he can continue, but he does not have the coach's trust, and he will never again receive from me information that may be important. Zero tolerance. I don't know exactly why, but it was always something important to me and on several occasions, I had to use it.

A positive fact, one of the players on the USA National Team worked for a company that produced material for the space industry (satellites, etc.). One day during an informal conversation, I asked him what he did at work and his answer was: "Javier, if I tell you what I do, I have to kill you." The fact is that this answer is half serious and half joke. I can confirm there are things that do not happen only in the movies, and my friend certainly did not tell me what he did for work.

INTRODUCTION TO A NEW JOB

In the chapters written so far, we've talked about the past, what has happened in each place I've worked. In each scenario, there was a beginning. That is, there was a present that had to prepare the future. They hired me. I would get there and start working. What was he doing? How did it start? What was it that I left for later? Well, I always did the same thing. I always used the same ideas. Let's call it the strategic method.

Strategic Method: It is composed of four successive sections connected to each other. All of them are important.

1. Positioning
2. Planning
3. Execution of the Plan
4. Evaluation – Adaptation

POSITIONING

This basically refers to knowing where I am and what position I am in. For that I must collect as much information as I can regarding the equipment I need to train and all the circumstances around that could influence the operation and my work.

MY TEAM

Questions to consider:

- What team do I have? In what position did they finish last year? Watch videos, listen to opinions. How old are the players? What kind of life do they have? Where do they work? Study? If they work, what kind of work?
- Where do they live? With their family or on their own? Do they have a girlfriend? Are they married?
- In what position do they play? Play a lot or play little?
- How many goals did we score and how many did they score compared to other teams?
- How many days and hours do we train per week? Can it be varied? Quality, age, experience? What other facilities do we have? Weight room, meeting room, auxiliary court, or warm-up area, etc.?
- Who is the captain? Who scores the goals? Who are the better passers? Do we have a counterattack?
- Who are the good defenders and what position do they play?
- What staff do I have (assistant coaches, video specialist, goalkeeper coach, physical trainer, physiotherapist, delegate, etc.)?
- What is the medical protocol if a player is injured in training?
- If there is a surgical operation, who operates?
- What form of transportation will be used for travel?
- Financial situation, are players getting paid?
- From the board of directors who is close to the team and who does not appear?
- All information we collect can be useful in getting up to speed quickly.

EXTERNAL INFORMATION TO OUR TEAM

- Who do we play against? Who are our direct rivals in the league? Who is above? Who is below?
- Ask the media for any information external to our club that we think could be interesting.

Once all this information is obtained, I meet individually with each player to compare and contrast. For example: If a player played as a left back, but didn't defend and had to switch out for defense, why?

Two things can happen. He accepts the criticism and acknowledges he has to change or he could say that he can defend, but the coach chose to switch him out. If in my plans he defends, I have a good opportunity to provoke him and demand he show me he is capable of defending.

PLANNING

With all the information we collect from positioning and any other useful information, we can identify the pros and cons of our team. From there we go to the planning phase. This means to organize, prioritize, and distribute all the work I have to do with the team. To do this we separate strengths and weaknesses.

This allows us to prioritize what we should do first and what to expect. Logically we must maintain, and if possible, enhance our strengths and improve our weaknesses.

We also have to know how many days of training we have until the competition starts. How long does the competition last? How much time do we have between matches? This leads us to consider planning annually.

The annual plan—also called macro-cycle—must collect all the activities that are done during the year and the timeframes. Likewise, it could be part of a longer period in time such as a biannual plan (in national teams, World Championships every two years) or a quadrennium (Olympic cycle every four years).

In a club the annual and longer cycles can be related among many other causes to the duration of the contract that the coach has just signed, to the objectives the club would like to achieve based on specific dates, or to plan the promotion to a new division within a period of X years.

The longer the planning periods, the more careful we must be with not getting caught up in the details. There are many variables involved in planning, however short, but the multi-year plans run the risk of becoming a merely theoretical exercise given the number of things that can happen which can vary greatly based on results etc. Annual plans are often helpful in planning for and controlling events that we know will occur within three to four months.

For example, we plan the season in its entirety, and then we start in September with games every week. The team trains every day except the day after the match. In other words, we have controlled the day-to-day and weekly period. The moment we look at the calendar, there is a national team competition one week in November, so I have to register it in my annual plan and take action. My next steps are to lighten the work during that week or to increase it, depending on many factors.

Another example can be to look at the calendar and see where we are going to play. For example, for league play we face our rivals at the end of February. Once again, I have to prepare for this and ensure my annual plan covers those events.

I will tell a truthful anecdote. In the four years I worked as a physical trainer for Club Atlético de Madrid de Fútbol, we started the preseason in July and the league in September. We adjusted our weekly work for Sunday matches during the September–December quarter. There were two weeks of preseason, and the quantity and intensity of work was increased.

The most important plan is the weekly one. We call these micro-cycles. During the planning for these micro cycles, we have to implement all the concepts, skills, and deficiencies we identify in the positioning phase.

Let's be more practical. You are sitting at your desk preparing and planning the work of your first week of the first month of your work with a club. In the positioning you discovered the defense at 6–0 has problems in position two on the right, where a player who is not very strong plays. His defensive movements are not good, so he is usually late at 9m for both outside shooting situations and feints, but he has to play in the attack because he is our best chance to score. You may have discovered more problems in your team, but let's go step-by-step and try to solve or help this player. I would consider the following:

- How often should the team train per week? If time is available, dedicate 15–20 minutes to working players deficiencies in each training. Also consider dedicating an entire training to defense and create a plan for the defensive work needed.
- Another solution is to only have three training sessions, but no opportunity to devote time to individual work. So, when working 4:4 or 6:6, the individual player has the obligation to execute the tasks that are asked of him individually.
- With three weekly workouts another option may be for the player to come thirty minutes before or stay thirty minutes after training is finished.

The most important thing is:
- Let the player see the effort you are making to improve his contribution to the team.
- Make sure the work is done. One because he needs it, and two so he can see you will not compromise on playing quality.
- Logically, this work must be integrated into the rest of the team's work and can not interfere with the team's training. Furthermore, the weaker defender has to integrate into the group that is playing defense. Since you need him to play in attack, there has to be time when he works on defense.

I purposely wanted to highlight a situation complicated by the lack of time and training to say there are almost always solutions for everything. As coaches, we have to recognize what each player needs, coordinate it with what others need, and create an environment and a learning dynamic that is constantly stimulating their motivation. At the same time, we combine their effort to improve individually with the connection the individuals have to play as a team.

Everything talked about so far refers to helping one player. Remember you have eighteen on the team and you have to be fair to all of them. Everyone has to have the feeling you are tending to their needs individually and collectively, that is to say that *you are their coach.*

Is it difficult? Yes. Is it possible? Yes. Also, you can always use the second trainer to work with the individuals who need more than you can provide.

There is a third cycle we call meso-cycles, which are made up of several micro-cycles (several weeks). It is about splitting the macro-cycles into several parts thus subdividing the season into several periods, and being able to distribute the work throughout the year with more precision and clarity.

For example, we have already scheduled the annual macro-cycle. In a general way we cover the events and situations that will surely occur and others that might occur.

We also have scheduled the micro-cycles, where we specify what we do on Monday, what we do on Tuesday, etc. A schedule needs to be created in advance to reflect changes even if they are only of quantity and quality of work, or to introduce new concepts the team needs.

In this example we are going to address the first four weeks (mid-July–mid-August). The competition begins in September, and we must reduce the physical preparation and begin to increase our technical and tactical skills. At this point in the planning, you decide it is necessary to continue with physical preparation to maintain everything else. If we enter the competition period, or you decide that even though the league begins on September 7th, you will do a meso-cycle of physical preparation in September and October to keep the physical preparation parameters in place from the preseason.

Another example could be what we talked about earlier concerning the competition the national team might have in March.

- Micro-cycle summary = 1 week
- Meso-cycle = 3–4–6 micro-cycle
- Macro-cycle = 2–3–6 meso-cycles

I am not trying to teach programming, but rather I'm saying in all the Federations and jobs I have worked during my professional career, I have always followed a plan.

It is important to know individual sports are different from team sports which means their programming has to be different. However, explanations and concepts I've given so far about planning are applicable to all sports.

How is it done? You know from the school of coaches what we must do is achieve and maintain a high bar in all aspects of physical, technical, and tactical skill every day of the week, and on Sundays (game days) have a peak in the graph as high as possible. It is difficult to control efforts, the weekly breaks, and the sequence in which we alternate the schedule with the faster but shorter efforts to give us the optimal shape when matches arrive.

In terms of organization and method, why not start the league in September defending 6–0 and at the same time make a three-month meso-cycle (September–December) preparing the team to defend 3–2–1 in the second round of the League.

Professor Seirullo, physical trainer of Fútbol Club Barcelona, is a perfect example to follow as he has provided the scientific quality to the concepts and methods of specific training in team sports. He applied these concepts and methods while he was in handball and football for Barcelona.

EXECUTION OF THE PLAN

It is time to start working. We have thought about both good and bad situations that can occur, so we must be alert to any complication or difficulty that could arise when we start the real work. Keep in mind to remain confident and positive in planning our strategies.

It is important to emphasize, although nothing in life is perfect or eternal, this is the plan we believe is the best way, so we must have patience and trust it.

EVALUATION

Following the line of the previous section, we must have a periodic and continuous evaluation over time that indicates whether we are on the right track or are moving away from our objectives. If this happens, we have to be flexible and quickly apply corrections to the original plan.

It is important to:
- Follow the plan we think is the best.
- Execute it with discipline and perseverance.

- Be attentive to the evaluations we make periodically and the results in the competition
- Make adjustments accordingly.

Programs and plans do not have to be complicated. The best plan is not the one that is the most complicated but the one in which the players feel acknowledged and capable of obtaining the best results.

LOS ANGELES '84

After the decision by the United States Federation to start training for the 1984 Olympics, in July 1981, a National Team Residency Plan was created, and we moved both the Women's and Men's Team to New Jersey. I started the program as the coach of both teams. This lasted until January 1982. During this time the Federation hired a Czechoslovakian coach for the Women's Team, and they went to live and train at the Olympic Training Center in Lake Placid, New York.

I stayed with the Men's Team in New Jersey. The eleven players rented out a house and later another house when five more joined. I moved with my family to Kendall Park, New Jersey, six miles from Princeton.

FEATURES AND OBJECTIVES

The main objective was to train daily and periodically have competitive matches:

- Players worked or attended classes at one of the many universities in the area during the day, and we trained at night (8:00–11:00 p.m.) in Fort Dix, New Jersey.
- We trained Monday to Friday in the evenings. On Saturday mornings we ran/did conditioning most weeks and rested on Sunday.
- Every month or two we went up to Canada on a weekend to play Saturday and Sunday games.
- Three times a year we traveled to Europe to play matches or tournaments in different countries.
- We worked with 18 to 21 players, and every July and December we did an evaluation. (It was actually continuous throughout the six months, and we also held tryouts for new players.) After the evaluation of training and matches of the players who were already in the program, and the possible new players, we decided who was still on the team and who would be asked to leave so we could bring in a new player to integrate into the team for the next six months.

We worked with twenty-one players (three for each position), although sometimes we had only two. There were some clubs with European immigrant players with American passports who could have been on the team, but they were not able to live in New Jersey. This excluded them since you had to be training in New Jersey with the group to be on the team that participated in the competitions.

There were also one or two players who played in Europe and who sometimes joined the team during a trip to play games (which aided in evaluating whether they would return next time).

When we went to Canada, we rented two vans. One for men and the other for women. We would leave New Jersey on Friday afternoons when players finished work or studies. We drove until we were near the border and rested for the night. The next day, Saturday, we arrived in Quebec or Montreal at noon just in time to eat before playing one or two games and finishing our trip with another game or two on Sunday morning. The last game finished by two or three in the afternoon. Then we would shower, eat, and travel back to New Jersey where we arrived around two or three in the morning, so on Monday we could maintain work or college schedules. On those weekends we rested on Monday and sometimes Tuesday, and we would see each other on Wednesday for normal evening training.

Travel to Europe was also quite an experience in the years 1981–1982. The cheapest way to fly to Europe from the East Coast was as follows: New York to Reykjavík, Iceland. We stayed 2–4 days and played 2–3 matches.

Icelandair only had flights to Europe from Reykjavík to Luxembourg where we boarded a bus that we normally contracted with the German Federation. It took us through Germany, France, Austria, and Switzerland, wherever we had organized matches. Sometime later, depending on where the matches were, we made different trips. For example, Denmark, Sweden, Norway, France, Spain, Portugal, Slovenia, Italy, Croatia, etc.

The trips lasted two to three weeks and we played as many games as possible. The record in the three years is fourteen games in seventeen days. We arrived at our destination at noon, ate, rested, played, ate again, slept, and left early in the morning on the bus to the next town where we played the next game and repeated this schedule. If the distances were longer, logically the trips varied to be able to play and rest enough.

With time we began to be more selective and demanding when deciding against whom we played. We looked for higher level tournaments against other national teams or first level clubs.

At the beginning of May 1984, or three months before the start of the Los Angeles '84 Olympiad, the USA Federation accepted my recommendation and hired Jordi Álvaro, who joined the group in Austria where we started our tour of several countries during those three months until we returned to the USA twenty days before the Olympics. Jordi did a great job. The players really liked his work and suggestions and found in him a calm counselor who complemented my work very well.

For me it was also a great help in working with the team, and on a personal level, it kept me calm thanks to our daily talks about the team. Although we also had some scares. Like the day in Germany we went for a run, and without realizing it, we entered a military zone and had to sprint when we heard nearby noises of tanks moving and firing machine guns.

This long journey took us through the following countries. We started in Austria and then in this order we went to Slovenia, Italy, Romania, Germany, and finished at an International Tournament of Spain in Barcelona.

These competitions and trips alternated with the official competitions of the Pan American Federation, so we played the Pan American Championships in

Manaus, Brazil, Buenos Aires Argentina, and Colorado Springs, USA during the three years of preparation.

In the early '80s, the Pan Americans' strongest teams were Canada and Cuba. As time progressed, the USA program was going up, Canada was going down, Cuba remained, and Brazil, Argentina, and Mexico began to appear. At the end of the Olympic program in 1984, the residency program ended and we began a period of preparation (non-residency) for the Pan American Games in Indianapolis in 1987. Working with most of the same players, the top two teams were Cuba and USA. In the final before 6,000 spectators, we beat Cuba in overtime which was the best result of USA handball until then and won the team Qualification for the Olympic Games in Seoul 1988.

During the build up to the 1987 Pan American Games, players participated with their clubs in some of the local and regional tournaments organized throughout the country. There was a very important competition for us called the National Sport Festival organized by the Olympic Committee—a kind of mini Olympics with all the Olympic sports. The country was divided into four regions (north, south, east, and west), and all traveled to the city where the competitions were held where they trained one week and played each other the following week.

For the Federation and for me, it was very easy to see the best players. I chose them and selected them to go work with us during the residency program in New Jersey every time we made changes to the team in July and December.

The plan we executed in New Jersey from July 1981 to July 1984 was a difficult situation for the players. Combining their personal lives (studies, jobs, family, etc.) with the training schedules wasn't easy.

We had the gym in Fort Dix where we trained from eight to eleven at night. When we had the two teams training, we shared the time. An hour and a half each plus half an hour warming up outside the court while the other team trained.

When the girls went to Lake Placid, we had three full hours for the men to train.

Monday, Wednesday, and Friday we did bodybuilding work with weights for an hour and then we did two hours of tactical-technical training. We finished at 11:00 p.m. The journey back home was roughly an hour or more depending on traffic. This schedule was normal for most of the team except for three players.

Bob Djokovich and Tom Schneeberger were technical engineers. Both graduates of the Air Force Air Academy. They had good jobs as electronic engineers in the space industry (satellites, etc.) in Colorado Springs.

They found work on Wall Street in Manhattan, New York thanks to Mike Lenard. The three lived together in another house near the team's home. The schedule for these three players was as follows:

- They began their work in Manhattan at 8:30 a.m.
- They left home at 7:00 a.m. and drove twenty minutes to the train station.
- The train to Manhattan was about sixty minutes.
- They worked from 8:30 a.m.–4:00 p.m.
- They returned on the train for one hour, and took the car to the house (twenty minutes) where they arrived more or less at 6:00 p.m.
- They ate something and drove to Fort Dix, sixty minutes, or seventy-five minutes (arrival about
    7:30 p.m.).
- They trained from 8:00 p.m. to 11:00 p.m.
- They returned home and arrived around 12:30 a.m.
- Eat, sleep, and "tomorrow will be the same day."

All this for three years. The Federation only paid for travel, medical services, and insurance. The rest was up to the team like housing, meals, and more.

I wanted to record this information so that it is understood a little better what this program meant for all of us who were involved, and to pay a small tribute to all these players who participated to a lesser or greater extent. Those who endured from beginning to end and participated in the Los Angeles '84 Olympiad, and those who fell by the wayside, who put forth effort but did not succeed. To all of them, my greatest admiration and my total gratitude for how much I learned as a coach and as a person during this time.

It marked the rest of my life. I had the opportunity to compete in many countries with teams of different categories. The work and coexistence with this group of people and direct evolution as handball players to face the difficulties of playing one day, for example, against a team of the second Bundesliga of Germany, and be lucky to be able to use that match as preparation. Because two days later we played the first match of a four-team tournament and the first match was against the USSR team.

The closeness and connection I had at that time with this group extends to this day and the mutual respect we have is evident. It is my intention to share some of the many anecdotes and behaviors I had the opportunity to experience.

It was important during this time, to have the evaluation process and the ability to change players two times a year in December and July. I believed in the group atmosphere of healthy rivalry and competition. In the USA, the process of entry and exit of the team—the selection or exclusion of a player is much more complicated than in Europe where the coach gives the list and the matter ends. In the USA (yes, as a coach), I give the list, but then above me I have the Selection Committee with whom I have to meet and explain and clarify any question or doubt they may have about the inclusion or not of a player on the list. And once the meeting is over, the Selection Committee announces the final selection of the team.

The player may appeal to the committee regarding his non-inclusion on the list. From there, the player has the right to a hearing of his case with the Selection Committee which confirms the final decision to include or exclude the player.

If the player is not satisfied and believes the decision is unfair, he can go to the Appeal Committee of the Olympic Committee, then to the ordinary courts, or in very special cases to the International Arbitration Tribunal of the Olympic Committee.

All this bureaucracy is one of the differences between the work of a coach in the USA versus the work in Europe, which is undoubtedly more work, and in many cases, an unnecessary complication. At the same time, it keeps you alert and demands concentration and seriousness when it comes to selecting the players for the national or Olympic team. People spend a lot of time and work as well as dedication and sacrifice for the chance to play on the national team or participate in an Olympic Games, and in no way should you take the team selection lightly.

To facilitate my work and reduce a little anxiety and emotional shock from informing a player he had to leave the team, a month prior, more or less, I spoke individually with the two or three players who were on the tightrope and communicated the situation. I explained their deficiencies and why I thought it was no longer necessary for them to remain on the team, so they had a month to prove me wrong. When the time came, I communicated the decision to the player that he had to leave the team or could continue with it.

As in all teams there was a core group of players who formed the compact group of the most talented players. Experienced people whose positions on the team were secure. At the other extreme there were always those two or three who were the number 17–18–19 of the group of twenty or the 15–16–17 of the group of eighteen.

As coaches we have an obligation to take care of and treat the two groups equally. There were tense and sometimes difficult moments, but this is what coaches are for. It gives dignity to our work and is what one may feel most proud of when over time you realize you were the coach and had to make those decisions.

RESULTS IN THE MATCHES OF THE OLYMPIAD LOS ANGELES '84				
	GAME SCORES			HALF-TIME SCORES
Germany	21	USA	19	(12–8)
Sweden	21	USA	18	(10–6)
Denmark	19	USA	16	(8–7)
Spain	17	USA	16	(10–9)
Korea	22	USA	22	(12–12)
USA	24	Japan	16	(9–5)

USA Team 1984 Olympics

Men's Team Handball

U.S. Loses to Spain by One Point

By TOM HAMILTON,
Times Staff Writer

The frustration of a winless 1984 Olympic record continued for the underdog U.S. men's team handball squad Monday as the Americans lost their fourth game to Spain, 17-16, in front of another capacity crowd of 3,300 at Cal State Fullerton.

And, while U.S. athletes in virtually every other Olympic sport continue to collect medals, the men's team handball squad is pondering what might have been.

"We've spent many hours and stayed up late at night asking ourselves why we can't win," winger Joe Story said. "Three months ago we played the same teams, and although we didn't win, we knew we were close." The U.S. team is ranked last among the six teams in Group B.

"Maybe we came in here thinking we were a little better than we are. I don't know. Maybe the next group of guys will win the same type of games we're losing in four years. It's all so frustrating." Story said.

Granted, Story and his teammates realized the inexperienced U.S. team had little more than a prayer to win against the top teams in the world at the 1984 Summer Games. After all, it was only a year ago that they were losing by 10 to 15 goals against the world powers.

But, U.S. Coach Javier Garcia Cuesta was highly optimistic following his team's performance in Romania in June, when his team lost to the highly touted Soviet Union by only two goals. Now, the

JAYNE KAMIN / Los An

Spain's Agustin Milian goes to the floor between two American players who try to prevent Spain's 17-16 victory in men handball competition Monday in Fu

memories of Romania seem very far away.

The United States opened an early 6-3 lead against Spain Monday when Story scored on a breakaway after a steal. That elusive first win looked promising until a defensive breakdown cost the United States six goals in about a six-minute span in the middle of the game.

In the first half, Bob Djokovich scored for an 8-6 lead, but Spain countered with four goals in the final five minutes, including one by Cecilio Alonso with 49 seconds left. Alonso's goal enabled Spain to take its first lead, 10-9, and it never trailed again.

Alonso opened the second half with a quick goal, and teammate Julian Ruiz added another. Suddenly Spain was holding a 12-9 lead.

After the game, Spain's Manager Juan Roman praised the United States, saying it's only be a matter of time before the United States emerges as a world power in team handball.

"What America has accomplished here is a triumph of work and sacrifice," he said. "With the growing number of clubs and players competing in American universities and (with) the talent available, it will be a very short time before America can beat quality teams."

Denmark 26, Sweden 19
ing its best game since th Cup seven months ago. D never trailed and snapped game losing streak to rival in international competition

The win set up a showd West Germany on Wed with the winner going o gold-medal game on S

Romania 28, Japan 22
Stinga scored 11 goals as c te Romania rebounded sluggish first half to down Japan.

Romania, 4-0-0, will pla slavia, 3-0-1, in Group A Wednesday.

We finished in ninth position.

BARCELONA '92

In June 1989, I finished my work with the Teka Santander club, and I joined my new job in the Spanish Handball Federation as Technical Director and Men's National Team Coach. In the following months I had to execute several previously scheduled activities including the organization and participation of our Junior Men's National Team in the Junior World Championship in Galicia '89.

Friendly matches against Russia were also scheduled in Leon, which was my first contact with the Men's National Team, coupled with a short visit to the youth programs (children and cadets) that were held annually during the summer.

The time I spent in Pamplona and Galicia assisting Cruz María Ibero in preparation for the juniors participating in the Galicia '89 World Championship, helped me to know the players who played the final against the USSR in Pontevedra.

The end of summer and autumn were very formative months for me as Technical Director. Due to the changes in the Federation, we had to redo the budgets and all the activities of all the national teams (including junior, youth) male and female, in addition to the Base Program and the identification of male and female talent. This was possible with the help of the staff of the Higher Sports Council, the ADO, and the Spanish Olympic Committee. In view of the new funding, we were able to financially support the activities and personnel involved and reform all programs of the technical area (in some, adding more training camps and players). And above all, we were able to design the guidelines that would serve as preparation for the Men's and Women's Olympic Teams.

It was an intense and very formative couple of months. Paco Sánchez was in charge of the women and I of the men. Mary Carmen and Chefi, our secretaries, put everything in black and white and together they finished the work plans of all the teams for the next three years including the Olympics.

These plans were presented to the directorate of the Federation, the Higher Sports Council, the ADO, and the Olympic Committee. After the programs were approved work could begin.

García Cuesta exige entusiasmo por encima de todo

PLAN 1989–1992 MEN'S NATIONAL TEAM PLAN

In developing the plan, I knew it would have to be consensual. I was very clear that I had to avoid entering into the dynamic of discussing the time dedicated to the national team and the time dedicated to the clubs. It would be a waste of energy and a confrontation that would get us nowhere.

We all knew it was impossible to satisfy both parties 100% because time was limited. There were several competitions between both the clubs and the national team. Since the players had their limits, it was necessary to introduce adequate rest times if we wanted them to be in optimal shape.

I knew despite the importance of Barcelona '92, the players could not give their full dedication to the national team. On the contrary, in other countries, clubs do not have the relevance they have in Europe and specifically in Spain.

The plan had to be based on the good work done in the clubs—maintaining the players in optimal, or as optimal shape as possible during the periods played by the national league or the international club competitions during the breaks. Specifically dedicated to the international competitions, the teams made sure to take advantage of any time we had to prepare.

Yet, both the clubs and the national teams were not positioned to understand each other. Neither wanted to harm the other by imposing criteria and arguments. We had to share the time. We had to coordinate the work, efforts, and time the players dedicated to the club and the national team.

CALENDAR

The time dedicated each year to the national team would be as follows:

1. End of June–July, after the end of the club competitions and a rest period we would have a preparation time. It began with physical tests to verify the physical condition of the players at the end of the club season, and it would end with an important competition on the same dates in which the Olympic Games were to be held, and with similar adversaries or the same ones we might face in Barcelona '92.

2. In October, we held a short training camp, a few days of training, and one or two friendly matches, or the German Super Cup when appropriate. We also did physical tests (control at the beginning of the club season and design of individual plans of the players with a view to work in December–January).

3. December–January, International Tournament of Spain (four teams).

4. February–March, World Championship when applicable or a competition such as the World Cup in Sweden.

5. Around Easter, a small training camp for training tactics, teamwork, coexistence, and physical tests.

131

The real activities that were carried out were:

- July 1989: Matches against the USSR.
- October 1989: Training-physical tests, friendly matches.
- January 1990: International Tournament of Spain.
- 28 February–10 March, 1990: World Championship in what was then known as Czechoslovakia, after matches in Austria.
- July 1990: Goodwill Games in Seattle, USA, after preparation with matches in the USA.
- October 1990: German Super Cup.
- January 1991: International Tournament of Spain.
- July 1991: Pre-Olympic Tournament in Granollers after preparation with matches.
- October 1991: German Super Cup.
- December 1991: Spanish Tournament.
- January 1992: World Cup in Sweden.
- June 1992: Preparation.
- 27 July–8 August: Olympic Games in Barcelona 1992.

All these competitions logically had their training periods and friendly preparation matches.

COLLABORATION WITH THE CLUBS

The philosophy was clear: talk to the club coaches and coordinate the individual work that could be needed, or the amount necessary to ensure all the players of the Olympic group avoided injuries and were in the best condition to perform at their best both in the club and on the national team.

Now, we all knew this would be very difficult to achieve. The planning and preparation for each team had to be different. The clubs played one game per week for eight months, and the national team played seven games in ten days. The work of preparation had to be different and the only way to combine all this was if the player had a good physical condition that allowed him to recover well after intense training or games. Through technique, tactics, and specific handball training, we got to work with adequate intensity and speed to build the form necessary to be able to compete at the highest level in handball. The national team player needed to increase the volume because the workload in a World Cup was significant. I want to add a concept that is one of the most important jobs of a coach, which is to have the players in good physical condition. The players also have to bring out a series of psychological aspects and we coaches help with this also.

Consider the following as an example of how you can orchestrate your plan:

- Player attitude = predisposed and prepared for everything.
- Player motivation = "I want to do well. I want to win (because of fame, honor, money)."
- Preparation by the coach = technical-tactical work and the players' trust will give them success.
- Help them during the match with an intelligent and positive plan and good coaching:
    a. The role for each player.
    b. The duration of the effort we ask of each player.
    c. The time of lower intensity between each decisive action in attack or defense.
    d. Substitutions with a rest for a few minutes on the bench.
    e. Changing the defense or attack.
    f. The rotations of players. Excluding a player from a game and giving him rest or sometimes the opposite. Planning micro-cycles or meso-cycles to make progress in deficiencies the player may have—rehabilitation of injuries, etc.

The end of all this leads us to the fact that the player has to be able to play and play well. Even when the player is relatively tired, their attitude, motivation, desire, and the training has to allow them to excel and will lead to maximizing game performance and achieving victory. Although the physical and technical levels will greatly improve the attitude and motivation, training and work habits are fundamental.

For Barcelona '92, since the players would spend most of their time in the clubs, it was important they worked well and when they arrived at the national team, there were no injuries or other problems that would prevent or diminish their capacity and contribution to the team.

It also had to work in reverse. When the activity with the national team ended, the players returned to the club in good health and happy with their performance, and after a break were motivated to work. At this point I can say with great satisfaction the work done by our medical services with Dr. Gutierrez at the head, followed by our beloved physio Pedro Mora, was excellent.

To help the plan, we include collaboration as an important part. Coaches along with the players on the national team were given monthly stipends. It was like this for several months until I received the order to eliminate those payments due to the complaints the clubs presented to the Federation.

As I mentioned before, all the preparation competitions during these three years were preceded by a more or less short training period—depending on the time of year, the calendar of club competitions, and the periods reserved internationally for the national teams.

Autumn (October–November) and Spring (March–April) were shorter. Seven to ten days with tactical training. If possible, a tournament (German Super Cup) and physical tests.

In the winter (December–January) there were longer training periods, finishing in the Spanish tournament or the World Cup in Sweden.

Summer training lasted several weeks, where there was a break after finishing the league and Copa del Rey and culminated with a great tournament on the same dates as the Olympiad.

- July 1990: Seattle, USA. Goodwill Games.
- July 1991: Pre-Olympic Tournament in Granollers.
- July 1992: Barcelona 1992.

For these competitions, the training camps were several weeks and divided into blocks.

BLOCK A:

- Twelve days (work morning and afternoon from Monday to Saturday noon, and rest Saturday afternoon and Sunday).
- Mornings: General physical preparation work, continuous running, fartlek, hills, flexibility breaks, Tuesday, Thursday, and Saturday.
- Monday, Wednesday, and Friday bodybuilding (weights in gym). We finished the session with passes and ball games in the gym.
- Afternoon: Tactical-technical work on the court.

BLOCK B:

- Twelve days (four sub-periods of three days and five sessions).
- Morning–afternoon, morning–afternoon, morning–rest, and repeat until twelve days.
- Mornings: Weightlifting is maintained and alternates with an endurance program on the athletics track. Monday, Wednesday,

and Friday = weightlifting Tuesday, Thursday, and Saturday = endurance.

- Afternoons: Technical-tactical work on the court.

BLOCK C:
- Twelve days (4+3+5).
- Tactical-technical and friendly matches (2–3). Tournament. Break 4–5 days.
- Official Competition: 1991 Pre-Olympic Tournament—1992 Olympiad.

To prepare for the '92 Olympiad, we trained in Jaca and went to play matches in Austria and what was then known as Czechoslovakia. The next block we played in a Spanish tournament. The next block matches were against Iceland and since we were already in the Olympic Village, we played against Hungary for the last warm-up match.

Throughout this time, a documentary was created recording all of our work. It was made in collaboration with the INEF of Galicia under the direction of Professor Gabriel Torres Tobío, and made available to the Federation for dissemination.

THE PLAYERS

Under the same philosophy of collaboration with the clubs, we had to integrate the players, make them aware of the need to work well in their clubs, and inform them of the program we had designed for the next three years so that they could organize their lives.

Naturally, players had the responsibility of playing well with their clubs since this would determine their selection to the National Team.

Once this happens, entering the National Team program you have to prepare to execute at the highest level of demands for both programs.

When I prepared the three-year strategic plan with a goal to get to Barcelona '92, the first thing was to review my notes and ideas about positioning. I asked myself, "What team do we have?" Cecilio, Uría, Novoa, Puig, Serrano, Juan de la Puente, and many more were great players and were worthy representatives of their generation. They gave many days of glory to our sport. At the same time, the new generation of juniors who had played in the final of the Galicia '89 Junior Championship had shown they legitimately belonged to the elite group of junior players worldwide.

Therefore, we had two generations. One who had already proven their worth throughout their long careers and had already had their Olympic opportunity.

On the other hand, we had a group of talented young players who stood out in their junior category and went into adult competitions. Intermingled between these two groups were others who were no longer juniors, however they still had a lot to give.

This positive and promising situation was undoubtedly due to the great work done for years before and continues in our days by the Talent Detection Program, carried out by the base handball department of the Spanish Federation.

With three years ahead and this group of players, we decided we would have to apply, once again, the fundamental principles regarding the work of the coach:

1. You always have to get the best immediate results.
2. When you leave, you have to leave the team in a better situation.

Select:
- Twenty-one players.
- Three for each position. But it would always be one experienced player and two young players.

The veteran "guarantees" the experience, and the young man has to show he deserves to be on the team.

These twenty-one players would be the recipients of the ADO scholarship. The selection at the beginning does not mean the security of the position. Only the best can be selected and there is a permanent evaluation of their performance. At any time, a player can be discharged and replaced by another on the ADO list. Injuries were also contemplated and depending on the severity, there were waiting periods for full recovery and continuity on the list.

The philosophy of collaboration with club coaches was also a player responsibility to comply properly on both fronts. He had to play well and be one of the best in the country to be selected. And he had to meet the requirement of extra work when he had to cover the commitments of the national team.

As we did with the coaches, in terms of work and salary, the players received a bonus payment for passing tests we periodically programmed. The work and objectives provided marks they had to pass.

Everything I have described so far tries to explain our intention and our goal of achieving a good result, and if possible a medal in Barcelona '92. We had three years to get the veterans to maintain their level and amalgamate with the young people who had to prove they deserved to be on the team and that we had not made a mistake by selecting them.

In general, no one was ruled out (veteran or younger player) even if they were not on the list at the beginning. Any player could be changed at any time. During the Olympics we gained an understanding of those who most deserved it based on their performance, attitude, desire, and motivation. Players could prove themselves during training, matches, and while in the preparation program.

I don't care about the age or the experience or quality the veteran had in the past or the lack thereof from the new players. The present is what mattered most. They had to show me which of them contributed the most to the team and who was the one who excelled in training and matches from here (1989) to July 1992. It was said there were too many new players who joined the team. Some of the veterans even came to me claiming they could not participate full time in the training but they could look for a way to be available at the end for the competitions.

Obviously, I did not accept this. I made one of our best players see that despite being one of the best, if not the best in his position, I would not have him if he did not attend the entire preparation program.

The entire plan was executed between 1990 and 1991. The team exceeded expectations, and we finished in fifth place at the World Championship in what was then known as Czechoslovakia in March 1990. We were third in the Goodwill Games behind Yugoslavia and the Soviet Union in July 1990. In the pre-Olympic Tournament of Granollers in July 1991, we were second, losing the final against the Soviet Union in overtime.

In the autumn of 1991, we won the German Super Cup where all the big teams always participated.

In January '92, we were third in the World Cup in Sweden against all Olympic rivals. These results, the training and good mix that occurred between the veteran players and the young players made us feel optimistic for the last part of the Olympic preparation and finally the Barcelona '92 Olympics.

THE OLYMPIC COMPETITION

The entire team (players and staff) felt confident coming into the competition. Maybe we had to admit the USSR had shown it was the main favorite and also Sweden was one step ahead of us.

It was the Olympics, so there were no easy rivals. All the teams were at the highest level, but we were as well.

In the two years prior to the Olympiad, we did not have the opportunity to play against Sweden because the two Federations held their international tournaments on the same dates—taking advantage of the Christmas period. We invited them to the Spanish tournament and they invited us to theirs two or three times. I called Daniel Costantini or he called me to anticipate the mutual invitation, but neither of us changed the dates of the tournaments, so it was not possible. The most I got was to see them in a tournament in Marseille in 1990, and a match in Paris two months before the Olympiad.

Selección Española de Balonmano. 14-1-92. Foto: Luis Gené.

The groups were established as follows:

GROUP A)	Sweden – Iceland – Korea – Hungary – Czechoslovakia – Brazil
GROUP B)	USSR – France – Spain – Romania – Germany – Egypt

Only the most crucial part remained—the selection of the players that would form our Olympic Team. This was never easy to do, but it had to be done. When I look back and reconstruct the moment of the decision of whether or not to select Oscar Grau, I think, maybe I was wrong because our 6–0 open defense was weaker without Oscar, which caused us to defend more time at 5–1 (our second defense).

It was possible we would lose the defense, but I risked it by believing we would win the attack with the other two pivots. If we look at the numbers after the fact, this was not the case at all. On defense, we conceded ninety-eight goals and we scored ninety-seven. The two teams from our group who went to the semifinals were USSR and France. Their goal counts were:

USSR:
- Goals for = 121; Goals against = 98

France:
- Goals for = 111; Goals against = 98

The other teams in our group gave up more goals.
- Romania = 115 - Germany 103 - Egypt 113

But on attack they scored more goals than we did. We only scored ninety-seven and our goal difference in the preliminary phase was -1.

The other teams scored as follows:
- Romania = 107
- Germany = 97
- Egypt = 92

The numbers were clear. Our problem was not defense, our problem was the attack. We did not play well in attack, and our first line did not play well in the organized attack.

Our first lines did not perform at the expected level considering what was done in the previous two years. Only Melo—who during the preparation had worked only in defense and counterattack—ended up being our most effective left back. In defense, Lorenzo Rico was our best performing player.

France beat us in the first game 16–18 (7–7). Then we won the other matches of the group (except for USSR), but France also won them, so we were third in the group. Therefore, we were outside the semifinals. We played in the 5th-6th place game against Korea which we won 36–21 (18–10), so we finished in fifth position.

We all expected more based on what was achieved during preparation, but in the competition we were not good in the key moments. The first match against

France was decisive. They managed to maintain and take the advantage in our group by defeating us.

For us, that match marked and weighed down our participation. We had not gone further than the highest finish that had been obtained since the generation of the Masip, Garralda, Urdangarin, Marín, Luis García, Franch, Urdiales, Barrufet, and Hermida. (How much I felt and how much I missed Chechu Villaldea who was removed from the team by his knee injury.) This generation of players competed with Melo, Cabanas, Julián, and Rico. But those who came after took over and gradually raised the level and quality until we managed to achieve World Champions in 2005 and 2013, bronze medals in Atlanta 1996, and Beijing 2008, and what will come after.

The most valuable consequence I took from this experience besides the honor of having been there, was the conviction and confirmation that you always have to position yourself, know where you are and what you have, plus you have to have a plan. Furthermore, you have to execute it, be patient, and evaluate it regularly, and be flexible to make the changes that may be necessary.

This structure, this feeling of organization is the best thing I have left of the wonderful moments I lived during my time in handball. Surely there will be other strategies, other ideas, and surely I have been wrong many times. However, I have always had a reference in my line and my plan, and I could always align and rectify as the situation dictated. When necessary, I was flexible when I needed to add or modify anything that came up after the initial plan was developed.

This confidence and sense of congruence, coupled with the unconditional support of my family, helped me feel a sense of accomplishment and continue my professional and private life, keeping things in perspective in the face of the diverse opinions.

MATCH RESULTS			
Spain – France	=	16–18	(7–7)
Spain – Egypt	=	23–18	(11–11)
Spain – Romania	=	21–20	(14–9)
Spain – USSR	=	18–24	(8–10)
Spain – Germany	=	19–18	(8–8)
Spain – Korea	=	36–21	(18–10)

EGYPT

ATLANTA PREPARATION 1996

On several occasions my Spanish and United States teams had played against Egypt. Since Egypt was one of the emerging countries, I knew the quality of the team. On one of the trips to Italy with the USA, I had the opportunity to chat for a couple of hours with Dr. Hassan Moustafa, the coach of Egypt, and Aziz Derouaz, the coach of Algeria.

What at first was just a normal conversation like many I had with many coaches when we were together in tournaments, became a fortuitous but important connection that later facilitated my entry as coach of Egypt in 1995.

Interestingly, Aziz Derouaz became Minister of Sports of Algeria for several years, and we crossed paths in several events, symposia, and congresses of the IHF.

As I said before, I knew a little about the players of the national team, but I was pleasantly surprised when I learned more about them. I was also pleasantly surprised by the facilities we were going to use at the Cairo Olympic Center, and the support we received from the Ministry of Bone Sports, the Government, and the Olympic Committee .

At that time handball was the second sport, which achieved the most international success for Egypt. The attention of the media was massive and television would broadcast live international competitions. It was impressive. During games the streets of Cairo were empty, and everyone was in front of the TV.

All this publicity placed pressure and responsibility on the shoulders of the players, which they handled very well. The economic compensation they received if they won, which together with their work, and the money they received from their clubs allowed them to have an economic situation above the average citizenship.

All this to say the players were all "professionals" and would be, as long as they were fully dedicated to the national team. After collecting all the information I needed about the program regarding the way the national team trained before my arrival I understand why they had so much success. Hence, I began to prepare a work plan.

WORK PLAN 1995–1996

The club league played on Fridays (a public holiday for Muslims) and they rested Saturdays. On Sunday we trained at night at the Olympic Training Center, and sometimes also on Sunday afternoon.

We trained Monday and Tuesday, morning and afternoon, and returned to the clubs to train Wednesday and Thursday. Then on Friday we played the club matches (I traveled, attended the matches, and made sure to always be attentive to the possibility of finding new players for the national team). The best teams were Zamalek and Ahly in Cairo. Alexandria and Port Said were where most of the players came from.

This weekly plan was applied throughout the year except for the two or three weeks we normally dedicated to the national team to train or have outside competitions, friendly matches, or tournaments as well as the official international competitions in Africa qualifying for the World Championships or Olympic Games.

I liked this schedule of work in the weekly microcycles because it allowed me constant contact with the players and at the same time there were not long periods of training that could cause chronic or mental fatigue.

On Mondays and Tuesdays there was a lot of basketball activity in the Olympic Center, and many weeks coincided with the work of the Junior Team, which facilitated my observation of players.

When it came to the Junior Team, they had a lot of training activities and matches plus a special regulation that made it easier for the clubs to work with them. For example, all the teams participating in the adult league had to also present a Junior Team during the first round of the competition. Just before the adult match, the Juniors' match occurred and the result counted for the adult league. The structure of two days of work per week was maintained all year round except in holiday periods or breaks after competitions.

The training habits were good. They were accustomed to training hard and intensely. The rules of conduct and discipline were not a problem facilitated by the sports culture and behavior and even religion (they do not drink alcohol).

TRAINING

There were not many changes in general, although individualized work (and working in groups) weight training was added depending on the competitions. The players welcomed the addition. Perhaps there was more reluctance from the coaches of the club teams and the Federation because they were not very accustomed to this type of work consisting of medium or high load weights.

In terms of technique and tactics, there was not much to change. They trained well and could execute any type of work assigned to them without a problem. The only issue that needed some time to adapt was the issue of open defense. As I mentioned in previous chapters, despite already knowing the fundamentals, it still took me a while to accept that we had a basic defensive position player in 12 m, another two in 9 m and three in 6 m, and all of them had the mentality of going forward to attack the ball.

In my first year of contract, before Atlanta '96, I think I managed to individually improve strength in the 1:1 thanks to the weightlifting program.

At this point, it was no hassle to adapt and apply any of my ideas or methods. They were a good team and due to the work done by Coach Tiedemann with the veterans, and Coach Gamal Shams over the junior team, the World Championship in 1993 turned out excellent. I paved a path, and I was ready for the next step.

The generation of Gohar, Ashraf, Mahmoud, Sherif, A. Agoushy, Hamada El-Ruby, had nothing to envy to the generation of Belal, El-Attar, Sameh Aldeluaty, and Ayman Salah. They all formed an experienced group and all year we kept alternating training in Cairo and trips to official competitions (African Championship in Zimbabwe), or friendly competitions such as the World Cup in Sweden—which we participated in almost every year since their coach Mr. Bengt Johansson was interested in playing against our defense to practice.

FIRST CONTRACT: ATLANTA 1996 (RESULTS)

We finished in sixth position. The best achieved until then by Egypt in an Olympic game.

ATLANTA 1996 (Results)	
Egypt - Algeria 19–16 (7–9)	Brazil - Egypt 20–31 (10–15)
Egypt - France 20–25 (9–12)	Egypt - Spain 9-20 (8–11)
Germany - Egypt 22–24 (9–11)	Egypt - Russia 26–29 (11–15)

SECOND CONTRACT 1996–1999

After the Olympic Handball Competition in Atlanta, the team returned home, and I stayed until the end of the Games. During this time, I met with Dr. Hassan Moustafa where we had the opportunity to talk, and as a result we reached an agreement for me to continue as coach for the next three years until the World Championship in Egypt 1999.

When everything was over and after a family trip in Spain, we returned to Egypt. Things were going well with my family. Linda started working at the American School in Cairo, our daughter continued her studies at the same school, and I began work for the new season.

I planned our year-round training calendar to reserve places at the Olympic Center.

We had long training sessions to prepare for the African competitions, and during these three years, we went to play in Benin, Tunisia, and South Africa.

We also had meetings about players, staff, times, and forms of training as well as game systems and especially defensive systems.

Some of these meetings were tense and at times they were difficult to manage. There were days I learned a lot because I had the opportunity to explain what we did last year, the reason, and expose the plans I had.

The feeling I had from those meetings from the beginning was that maybe some people in Egyptian handball did not expect me to continue after Atlanta '96, and definitely not for three years to the 1999 World Cup in Egypt.

There were two specific priorities I had during this time:

1.   Strength training work with weights
2.   Open defenses or "European" defenses

Some people on the coaching staff of the national teams were not very familiar with weight training and were not entirely convinced it was useful in any case. Nonetheless, in the end we continued to do the weight work.

The topic of defenses required much more time and discussion, but it was very interesting and a great lesson for me.

There I was in the middle of Cairo. In the offices of the Handball Federation meeting with four or five technicians of the Federation plus the head of the group, professor of the University of Alexandria, and an assiduous participant of the technical symposia of the IHF, discussing and deciding how we were going to defend.

After several days, it was decided our main defense would be open to working hard against the ball, but I would continue working the weight training in an effort to strengthen the 1:1 in all concepts—physical, technical, and individual tactics.

Regarding the collective tactics, we reached the conclusion we would defend very open with defenders attacking the opponent with the ball out to 10–11 m despite the distances and the large spaces this established. A minimum diagonal aid from side-to-side covering the pivot on the opposite side of the ball and working together with the outsiders and the second defenders coordinating to mark their opponent outside the 6 m, (either the two leave or the two stay but not one yes and one no). This would help us facilitate the 1:1 in attack.

The final solution was risky, but it was a delight to see the players move, communicate, and help each other defend in the zone (a deep area of 11–12 m), in the center, and the second defenders with great mobility attacking the sides of the other team with the ball, closing back on the opposite side of the ball to help the center in marking the pivot.

We started working and the training program and the competitions we played were practically the same throughout the second quarter of 1996 until May 1997.

RESULTS 1997 KUMAMOTO WORLD CHAMPIONSHIPS

CZECHIA - EGYPT 22–24 (11–12)	EGYPT - SPAIN 19–19 (11–10)
EGYPT - TUNISIA 24–18 (12–8)	BRAZIL - EGYPT 11–33 (4–18)
PORTUGAL - EGYPT 25–29 (14–12)	CUBA - EGYPT 20–24 (9–10)
EGYPT - FRANCE 19–22 (8–13)	KOREA - EGYPT 27–28 (11–15)
EGYPT - ICELAND 20–23 (9–10)	

We finished sixth, equaling the best ranking ever in a World Championship Cup.

After every major international competition, we always had a rest period. But it was also common for several of the players to receive offers, normally from European clubs, but also from the Emirates or Saudi Arabia.

The Egyptian Federation did not allow them to play outside the country which created psychological and motivation problems in those players and ultimately caused some anger and frustration that took them a while to overcome.

It happened several times with several players. A disagreement between the Federation and players would occur, prompting me to intervene, but after a couple of months they usually overcame it because at the end of the day, the situation they had in Egypt was not bad.

After the World Cup in Kumamoto, the same thing happened. Several players had offers, but in this case there was an additional problem. After the World Cup, we had the Mediterranean Games in Italy. It was not the best time for a new competition, and some players did not want to go back into hardcore training.

I spoke in the Federation and recommended for the Junior Team to participate. I was not very successful, and we had to go to Italy with a lot of displeased players.

In a game in which things were quite serious and difficult, I called one of the players from the bench to make a substitution. Based on the face he made and his body language, it led me to ask him if wanted to play or not, and he replied that he did not. After that moment he did not play anymore and the game continued. When I arrived in Cairo, I filed a report. The Federation punished him with six months of suspension of employment and salary, and he was not able to play with the national team or his club.

At the same time, I understood the player's frustration in regard to not being allowed to leave the country to play in Europe, but I could not allow that kind of behavior (remember the fundamental principles):

1. Attitude comes first.
2. The line of work is always maintained.

Time passed and we kept the same training plan at two days per week. At the end of the year something curious happened. We were training at the Olympic Center preparing for the World Cup in Sweden when I received a message that Dr. Hassan Moustafa wanted to talk to me. Dr. Moustafa informed me I had to leave the team because they decided to have another coach lead the team going forward (mid-December 1998 until June when the World Championships would be in Egypt).

As I explained in the section of my resume, I already had an agreement to work with Portugal once my commitment to Egypt was over. On a family level we would have to wait until June for our daughter to graduate from the American School and for my wife to finish the school year. The Federation's proposal was that I would have to leave the Men's National Team, but they wanted me to continue as coach of the Junior Team. I rejected the offer and I contacted Portugal and asked them when I should join. They answered as soon as possible. At home we had already decided that I would join my new job in Lisbon, and Linda and Cristina would stay until June to finish school and graduate.

Linda and I decided to board the "Nile cruise" everyone spoke of while Cristina stayed in Cairo. It was a total of three days of sailing on the Nile between Aswan and Luxor. At the end of the cruise my daughter told me the Federation called and stated they wanted me to remain on the team. I arrived in Cairo and met with Hassan Moustafa. They really wanted me to go back to coaching the team, informing me of the details of what happened.

Apparently, some players talked to Moustafa, asking him to get a new coach, which they did. They trained for a week and went to play the World Cup in Sweden. The coach who replaced me was Branislav Pokrajac, a great innovator and excellent professor in clinics and symposia who at that time was very involved in his ideas of taking a basketball approach to handball.

I won't go into judging whether or not it was the right thing to do. The fact is that on the way back to Cairo, Hassan Moustafa asked me to take the reins again. It was a strange feeling and despite the tension and stress the World Championship produced, and the responsibility that came with it, I was very calm and comfortable, and the last six months passed quickly. It was full of handball and all I had to do as a coach, though I had a list of tasks to complete.

1. Contact Portugal and tell them that again we had to postpone my start date until July after the World Cup.
2. Attend to and convince some of the players who had participated in the change of coaches that they had nothing to fear; that everything was fine with me. Though they expected revenge on my part, which of course was not going to happen, it took a while until they were convinced of it.
3. Prepare the move to Portugal.
4. Prepare for the final training phase before the World Cup.
5. Lead this special group of players and all the other people on the staff and the people from the federation offices who helped so much.

As a side note, the gift and inscription on the gift that Gohar gave me as team captain at the end of my contract has a very special place in my heart.

Before finishing this section with the results of the World Cup matches, I want to tell the coaches reading this that our work as coaches has, as you know, a little bit of everything. We have to teach and work on the technique, tactics, and the physical conditioning. We are forced to be psychologists, spiritual advisors, etc. I have learned all aspects of real life sooner or later come to light in sport.

I was left with good and bad memories, experiences, and culture shock. My quick adaptations to the circumstances allowed me to move forward with situations that would have been complicated if I had acted 100% with my emotions.

I had a continued goal of keeping the team together. I reminded them often to keep things in perspective and to not abandon their desire and ambition to be World Champions.

Dear colleagues, I conclude by saying that what allowed me to have such a good experience in Egypt and leave there with very special relationships with the people I worked with was:

1. Having common sense.

2. Having an attitude and consistency of work and behavior that everyone came to understand and accept.

Yes, with all the modesty in the world I can say that I do not know if I obtained the best possible results, but without a doubt the team was better when I left than when I arrived. And we all learned and improved in the process.

RESULTS 1999 EGYPT WORLD CHAMPIONSHIPS

We finished seventh which meant qualifying for the Sydney Olympics in 2000.

EGYPT - BRAZIL 28–19 (16–8)	CUBA - EGYPT 29–31 (14–17)
SAUDI ARABIA - EGYPT 16–19 (4–10)	EGYPT - GERMANY 18–23 (7–9)
EGYPT - MKD 30–24 (18–8)	TUNISIA - EGYPT 22–24 (13–14)
RUSSIA - EGYPT 26–20 (11–8)	EGYPT - CUBA 35–28 (15–14)
EGYPT - FRANCE 25–27 (22–22, 12:12) Overtime (7–9)	

PORTUGAL

The trip to Portugal had been brewing for a long time. I remember a conversation with Luis Santos and Carlos Cruz after a game we played in Mérida. I think it was my first time with the American team (1981–1984) in which we spoke about the possibility of me working in Portugal.

I had the opportunity to go to Portugal to give clinics in Porto, Lisbon, and Madeira, where I could verify the quality and training of the Portuguese coaches. Some of the players' skills were very exceptional. There was no reason for them to envy anyone, even those from Spain.

One of the reasons, perhaps the most important that influenced me and helped me decide, was undoubtedly the friendship I had with Luis Santos and Carlos Cruz. I have always had respect for their opinions in symposia or congresses of IHF or EHF.

Luis Santos is one of the few people who provided the best ideas about the future of handball in terms of a professional sport. Carlos Cruz was the calm "professor" who contrasted with the impetus of the president.

Once in Portugal, Henrique Torrinha was another person who helped me a lot to know the different, people, and regions of Portuguese geography.

I am also not able to forget Leonor, Miguel, and all the staff of the office. Together with many others who, on so many occasions and in so many different ways, helped my stay in Portugal be profitable, both professionally and personally.

I lived in Portugal for six years. Let's divide them into three stages:

1. Arrival and success in qualifying against Yugoslavia (We won one in Portugal and lost one in Yugoslavia).
2. Work preparation and execution of the Congress of IHF in Lisbon 2000, which decided the venue of the 2003 World Cup and election of the president.
3. Transition and organization of the 2003 World Cup and its bad result. We finished in twelfth place.

There were quite a lot of expectations about who would be the coach of the national team. It was rumored it would be me. The journalists who followed the World Championship in Cairo always came with the same question after each press conference: Is it true or not that you are going to Portugal?

Once the proper presentations and meetings in Lisbon were over, we started working because shortly after we had a qualifier with Yugoslavia for the European Championship in 2000.

There were three training camps of twelve days working with the following structure: Morning–afternoon, morning–afternoon, morning–rest. We repeated this microcycle four times to complete the twelve days.

The players were very motivated. The task was not easy because Yugoslavia, in general, was better than us. The team was used to planning an attack with more closed tactics than in Spain.

Victor, the nationalized Ukrainian center-back, was a great team manager, a great player, and a highly respected person in the group. Resende and Eduardo Filipe provided the scoring. They were players of international level. Andurinho, a left wing, had the athletic quality and improvisation. Filipe Cruz on the right side was our first left-handed player in that position, and all the players coordinated with Galambas, our pivot. When we started training, I realized our problems would come more from the defense than from the attack.

We lacked intensity, aggressiveness and anticipation in defense. It seemed as if defense was the time to rest and prepare for the attack. We could score goals against anyone, but we needed to decrease the number of goals conceded.

I came from four years in Egypt, accustomed to very open defenses, at first by inertia, and then because I saw we could use that point of extra energy and intensity that was needed to defend so openly. In Portugal, we did a lot of work in 3:3 but knowing our defense would primarily be 6:0 and 5:1, we hoped individual work would improve.

It was a very positive period for the team and for me. We played a great game against Yugoslavia in Portugal and won. Above all, we did a great job in the second leg in Yugoslavia especially in the last minutes. We were so close, but we ended up losing, but we still won the Qualifier.

This success was followed by a very good performance in the European Championship. However, the proximity to Spain and its world of handball produced a trend to imitate what the Spanish clubs did; without realizing they were not exactly an example to be copied.

EUROPEAN CHAMPIONSHIPS 2000 CROATIA 21–30 JANUARY 2000 RESULTS

PORTUGAL 28 - SLOVENIA 27	PORTUGAL 28 - ICELAND 25
PORTUGAL 21 - SWEDEN 29	PORTUGAL 20 - RUSSIA 24
PORTUGAL 26 - DENMARK 28	PORTUGAL 30 - NORWAY 27

We finished seventh.

The game we lost against Denmark (28–26) was the one we used 3:3. We were losing by eight midway through the second half. It was the last game of the group, and to beat Denmark in the standings we could not lose by three or more. We lost by two but we had better goals making us fourth in the group and Denmark fifth. So, we played for seventh and eighth, and Denmark played for ninth and tenth.

The start was certainly good. Never had Portugal come so far. Carlos Resende was named best left-back of the tournament, and the atmosphere was really optimistic and positive.

In 2000, the IHF decided to hold the congress in Lisbon. It was an important congress because there were elections for president, and for us it was also very important because the decision where the 2003 World Championship would be located was also on the agenda.

Frankly, I was impressed by the work the Portuguese Federation had done prior to the arrival of the congressmen. The team was formed by Luis Santos, Carlos Cruz, Henrique Torrinha, Leonor acting as visible heads, plus some other people responsible for different areas. I myself was involved in several important areas where key decisions were made.

THE RESULT

Portugal was chosen for the 2003 World Cup, and Hassan Moustafa was elected president. I think the presence of Portugal in the middle of the handball world with good connection with Central and South America was helpful. Also, Manoel Oliveira had managed to vote in block to which the Portuguese-speaking African countries joined. Europe was somewhat divided with the ex-communist block and the Nordics. It all worked out in Portugal's favor.

After the vote and selection at the Congress, we began the work of organization and realization of the World Cup. An organizing committee was created, and a house was acquired near the Federation. There were offices focused on organization directed by Carlos Cruz and that of the Technical Commission directed by me.

The Technical Commission was totally dedicated to our participation in the World Championship. Watching matches, scouting new players, and for a while training physically in Ajuda Park at noon with a group of young players with the typical training program of European countries.

As for the 2003 World Cup, the venues were designated. However, there were exasperating delays and multiple excuses for not having the facilities available and being able to train and become familiar with them. But in the end the World Cup went ahead. The facilities were ready; however it was the team that was not up to the task.

We qualified to play the World Cup in France 2001, with similar preparation, but something did not add up this time. We were OK to play, but it was one of those situations where you feel we could have done better.

RESULTS WORLD CHAMPIONSHIPS FRANCE 2001

PORTUGAL - CZECHIA 29–19 (14–10)	ICELAND - PORTUGAL 22–19 (10–11)
EGYPT - PORTUGAL 23–19 (9–10)	PORTUGAL - SWEDEN 25–32 (12–16)
PORTUGAL - MOROCCO 30–26 (11-13)	FRANCE - PORTUGAL 23–18 (10–10)

We finished in sixteenth place, and we left the World Championship 2001 with a bittersweet feeling. We returned to Portugal knowing we were still a good team, because in the end we lost the games we were expected to lose and won the games that we were expected to win.

For many years I have been convinced that the respect of certain people and officials who direct the tournaments is important when it comes to moving up the ladder.

We had it in Croatia 2000, when we beat Slovenia (28–27), Iceland (28–25), and finally Norway (30–27) to finish seventh. We should have had it in the 2001 World Cup when we played against the Czech Republic, Egypt, or Iceland, but we didn't have it, and we weren't the team we wanted to be.

All this gave me a lot to think about, and I came to the conclusion we needed something more. So after a while, I met with Luis Santos and later with Carlos Cruz and Torrinha, and we discussed that the team needed new blood. It was important for us to improve as quickly as possible in certain positions and prepare a group of young players for the European Championships 2002 in Sweden, and "our" World Cup in Portugal 2003.

At the meeting, I recommended we improve the Junior National Team and have a possible B selection of younger players, and that we hire Professor Manuel Laguna who was a great trainer of players in several clubs in Spain as well as coach of the Junior National Team of Spain. And if he was not the best, he was one of the best teachers of courses and clinics who was able to simplify through presentations, the ideas we all have in our heads, but are not able to express.

We also needed our group of players to stop idealizing and deifying our opponents, some of whom were their idols. We needed to convince them there was a time when these famous players were like them and that only the continuity and seriousness of their work had brought them success. We could have that same success.

It occurred to me that our goalkeepers, although good, would benefit from training with Mats Olsson. I knew him from my time at Teka Santander, and I knew he could contribute a lot to our goalkeepers but also as an assistant coach on our staff. His personality, knowledge, and experience would be a very good addition to our team.

At the end of the meetings, I was given the green light to contact Manuel and Mats, and the rest was history.

We qualified to play the European Championships 2002 in Sweden, and these were the results:

PORTUGAL 26 - ISRAEL 15	DENMARK 27 - PORTUGAL 20
RUSSIA 28 - PORTUGAL 19	UKRAINE 23 - PORTUGAL 28
R. CZECH 29 - PORTUGAL 27	SWEDEN 27 - PORTUGAL 22
PORTUGAL 31 - YUGOSLAVIA 25	

We finished ninth and looked ahead with a more positive feeling for the next great challenge that would be the 2003, home World Championship in Portugal. Beyond this, 2003 and 2004, were years to prepare and finish laying the foundations for an expansion of handball in Portugal. But as I explained in the first section of this book, there were often complaints or comments, some joking, some not about our plan and execution. It often felt like things were left unsaid because you could see a shift in attitudes and there was coldness regarding anything that came from the Federation.

We had a good generation of players, perhaps the best who were ready to explode in the 2003 World Cup playing at home. We could also qualify for the 2004 Olympiad. That's how it was planned; that was our goal.

Sadly, our goal was not achieved. The team did not play well, and we did not manage to excite spectators or create the festive atmosphere we needed to rise to the "top level". We missed the opportunity to raise the bar and lay a better foundation for the future.

Afterward, there were important meetings of the Federation, and also with clubs at the official level as well as informal conversations. The conclusions of the initial meetings led people to think there would be a national professional league under the protection and legal coverage of the Federation. At the last meeting, the clubs decided not to accept this new league because they wanted to create a new professional league outside the Federation.

I do not remember the dates of all these events, but suffice it to say the positive feelings and results from 2000 did not continue.

On a positive note, when Manuel Laguna and Matts Olsson joined the team, they gave us the touch we wanted. And further, we created the Junior's program with two groups of young people. One group was in Porto led by Manuel Laguna, and another in Lisbon led by me. We worked for a year, but after that the Federation considered the expense and the results (with new players) they could not justify the investment.

I will not dwell much more on the negative things, but the last two years of my stay and work in Portugal were always weighed down by the institutional and personal confrontation between the clubs, their league and the Federation which prohibited players from attending to the work of the national team. Added to this concept of confrontation between institutions was a personal issue—a clear attempt to remove Luis Santos as president. Things got worse and really the last year 2004–2005 was quite negative. A few months before the end of my contract I communicated to the president my intention not to renew and to accept the offer I had from Spain.

It was a bit turbulent for a few months with all the press and public opinion. We tried to focus on two things:

On one hand, the preparation of the national team for the European Championship in Slovenia 2004. Our qualification for this against Norway completed the cycle since Portugal qualified for all official competitions during the years of my contract. (Croatia 2000, France 2001, Sweden 2002, Portugal 2003, and Slovenia 2004). The second was the culmination of the Junior's program. We worked for a year, and some of the players who participated were later part of the national team.

I would like to finish this report on my work in Portugal thanking all the staff of the Portuguese Federation for their help and collaboration which made my job much easier. Of course, Mr. Luis Santos, an intelligent president with great ideas on how to turn handball into a professional sport governed by rules and principles. He knew how to implement the business structure with good results.

2005 TECHNICAL DIRECTOR – SPAIN

When I finished my work in Portugal, I accepted the offer from the Spanish Federation as Technical Director, so I transferred from Lisbon to Madrid to start my new job once again, assuming the role of supporting the national teams. In this case, I did not oversee the Men's National Team whose Technical Director and coach was Juan Carlos Pastor.

This time I got a little more involved in the work of the Talent Detection Program, and we did an exchange with Denmark. I went to Denmark and gave a speech on how we handled talent detection in Spain, and Professor Petersen, director of one of the academies in Copenhagen, worked for two days with our kids at the summer camp in our Base Program.

During my four years as Technical Director, a lot of work was done with the Women's Teams (top level, junior, and youth). We also communicated with various countries and created a strategy to provide competition at the highest level for our Women's Youth Teams, which was later expanded also to the men.

At the level of the Women's Team, changes were also made to bring on new talented players. Changes were made to the technical staff, and efforts were made to organize more friendly preparation competitions.

From the Higher Sports Council, we were asked for a work plan with a separate budget for males and females. We created the Nano Handball Program at the national level.

As always there was a good relationship between the Olympic Committee and its technicians, and the same with those of the council who greatly facilitated the common work and projects including the Olympic Games in Beijing 2008.

BRAZIL

With the result of the elections in the Spanish Federation, Jesús Ricondo had to leave the Federation and Juan de Dios Román was elected president.

I already had agreed with Brazil that if Jesús had to leave, I would serve as Men's National Coach and Coordinator of the Men's and Women's National Team programs, as well as the talent detection and training programs for Brazil.

Juan de Dios won the elections, and so I went to Brazil. The first year we lived in São Bernardo near São Paulo, which has the strongest nucleus of handball in Brazil. As always, the first thing was to position myself to study the landscape, and to determine the position we were in internally and externally. It took several months to clearly determine what our potential was and where we should focus our efforts.

In Brazil, we had a great advantage over the rest of the American countries. Handball was fully included in the Physical Education curriculum in schools which meant thousands of boys and girls were familiar with the sport and its strategies.

The relationship between handball and Physical Education goes even further. In Brazil, an essential requirement to be a handball coach is that you have to be a Physical Education teacher.

A second advantage is the annual symposium the Federation organizes where they invite all the handball teachers of the universities and schools of Physical Education throughout the country to spend a weekend meeting and attending talks and conferences regarding the latest advances and trends in handball in all concepts (physical, technical, tactical). It took us a while to plan and regulate all the activities in which my involvement was necessary, but in general we could divide it into a number of different parts.

The search for talent was already organized and directed in the South (Blumenau had good facilities) by Jordi Rivera. I proposed, once again, to the Federation to implement and apply the same Talent Detection Plan we used in Spain, which I consider one of the best in the world. It was about applying (in a slightly systematic way), the criteria we used in the Spanish Federation to choose, evaluate, and monitor all aspects (physical, technical, and individual tactics) of players at younger ages. Parallel to these activities, I taught several courses and clinics in different parts of the country.

The other great section of my work was the Men's and Women's National Teams. Brazil is one of the few countries in which the Women's Team was superior to the Men's team in terms of results, quality of players, work in the clubs, etc.

When I started meeting with the coaches of women's clubs, I immediately realized there was a reluctance coming from players. It was as if they were saying, "We know what we have to do." The truth was, in the past they had done well. Internationally the Women's Team was much more competitive than the Men's. Several of the Women's National team players played in European Clubs, though their team had many older players.

And there were many difficulties incorporating the players who played in Europe. Several training sessions were held in Praia Grande with the aim of incorporating some new players who demonstrated potential.

With an eye on the Brazil 2011 World Championship, we had many conversations regarding two players who played for Hypo Bank, Vienna. President Manoel Oliveira and I went to Vienna. We met with the leaders of Hypo Bank, and not only was the situation involving the two players resolved, but four others were added to the team, and several joint training sessions were carried out between the two groups.

The organization of the Women's World Cup was complicated because the State of Santa Catarina withdrew almost at the last minute. The Federation had to hastily organize the event in São Paulo with higher costs, more time pressures, etc. In any case, it served as a springboard for the World Cup in Serbia 2013, where the Brazil women ended up being Champions.

Of course, the Women's team had no strong competition on the American continent. Only Argentina presented a minimal threat to its superiority.

The Brazil Men's Team in the years 2009–2012, was a good team which was accustomed to intense work at the technical-tactical level. They had the ease and quality of play between the first line and the pivot as their most outstanding weapon. In general, players were accustomed to competing in the league with four or five clubs at the semi-professional level requiring their full dedication.

We also did a lot of work in training sessions and friendly matches in order to incorporate young players. And these days they are fully integrated into the national team as in the case of Thiagus, Fábio, and some of the new ones who were youth at the time I was there.

The global economic crisis began to affect Brazil and the sport was greatly damaged. The Federation was no stranger to these problems, but I can say the work of the directors, spearheaded by Manoel Luis Oliveira, led to very few technical activities being suspended.

The biggest problem I found with the team was the excessive rivalry and confrontation between Brazil and Argentina at all levels. For handball, it really meant a lack of control in stressful situations for players who were otherwise calm and intelligent.

The preparation work always ran well when we played against teams like Denmark, Iceland, Tunisia, and Egypt. We ended with good results and performances. However, when we came to head to head competition against Argentina, we were not able to play well. Only in the South American Games in Medellín, Colombia, did we manage to beat them. This feeling of not having been able to improve this deficiency the team had, at least under my direction, is one of the few negative things I still think about. When considering the competitions, I have always been very clear that:

1. First and foremost, you must win.
2. When you leave, the team has to be better than when you initially joined.

Of course, the former was not achieved much of the time, and in this case I am not quite sure I achieved the latter.

My work in Brazil ended in 2012, and I only have words of gratitude and respect for the people of the Federation whose work can only be described as extraordinary.

Previously I mentioned a very interesting project to which a lot of time was dedicated. Little by little the plans were finalized thanks to the effort of many people led by the president's commitment and the support of other authorities. It was about opening a training center in the city of São Bernardo where they would remodel and rebuild a Volkswagen company warehouse.

The center would consist of a complex with a sports pavilion, weight room, spaces for future research laboratories, conference rooms, and space to conduct updated courses for coaches and players. In addition to space for offices, as well as bedrooms and dining there was a view to housing the training camps for the national teams. I left before it was officially inaugurated. I do not know how it's being used today, but in its day, it was a milestone in the development of handball in Brazil and in the Americas.

The normal operation of this center will also allow a greater number of activities related to talent detection and development, which was a challenge when I was in charge due to financial problems such as cuts in the sponsorship of the Federation and the fact that we could not use the Blumenau facilities for almost a year and a half due to flooding which damaged the gym.

Brazil is a country with excellent structure and organization starting with the schools where handball is included in the daily activity through all categories of children, youth, juniors, and adults. The National League had well prepared, professional players competing at their respective competitions at all regional, state, and federal levels. And the Men's and Women's National Teams had their own preparation programs and competitions such as the Pan American Games, World Championships, and Olympic Games.

In recent years, many players have gone to play with European club teams in different countries. So much emphasis seems to be on finding ways to increase the potential of the national team in less time. But in my opinion, all Federations should have their Talent Detection Programs and continuously develop talent through competitions at all levels, culminating in the professional club leagues and the qualification and participation in the World Championships and Olympic Games. Brazil is the American country best positioned to achieve all these objectives.

REGIONAL WORK–RESIDENCY PROGRAM AT AUBURN UNIVERSITY ALABAMA

When I arrived in the United States to evaluate returning, we met and discussed the future direction and focus of the programs. At the end of the meeting, I reached an agreement to work with the Men's National Team.

The decision was more or less focused on searching out and developing new handball players in different parts of the country. We aimed to help and be a reinforcement for coaches and referees so they would have access to courses and updated material. We also had the possibility of helping with sports equipment (balls, goals, etc.).

Areas of focus we discussed were New York (in the city and in Long Island), Chicago, Colorado Springs, Los Angeles, San Francisco, North Carolina—places where developed programs already existed. The first year, 2012 and part of 2013, were dedicated to carrying out clinics and tryouts. The first one we held in Lake Placid, New York for both men and women was my first direct contact with players on the court, some of whom were a part of and could continue to be on the national team.

In the periodic meetings we had, we began to talk more consistently about the possibility of creating a residential program in which the group of previously selected players could train daily in addition to being able to study or work during the day.

It was about having one or more places in the country where we could work with new players and attempt to promote handball at all levels. The challenge, as always, was to put firm plans in place and secure everything necessary to execute such a program.

At this point, I was lucky enough to contact one of the players from the national team I coached in 1979–1980. I called Reita Clanton to see if she could help me find players since after leaving handball she had become a basketball, volleyball, and softball coach.

Our goal was clear—the formation of a residential program similar to those we had in New Jersey and Lake Placid from July 1981 to July 1984 and in Atlanta in 1995–1996.

Thanks to Reita's willingness, efforts, connections and countless meetings, David Gascon (USTHF Director in charge of the national teams), Reita and I met with the Department of Kinesiology staff at Auburn University in Alabama. An agreement was reached to create a residential program.

We could not have asked for anything better. The university provided us with a gym with capacity for 12,000 spectators—practically for our exclusive use—all medical services, doctors, physiotherapists, laboratories of physiology, biomechanics of the Department of Kinesiology, coupled with our willingness to perform tests as well as conduct research related to all these disciplines.

The players lived in rented apartments in the city, and we trained about eight times in weekly sessions from Monday to Friday. In the afternoon we did technical-tactical work, and three days in the mornings we did individual weightlifting, and technical work. We rested Saturday and Sunday unless we played a game against local teams.

We also had other benefits. For instance, players who studied at Auburn University were granted Alabama state residency which greatly reduced their tuition since they were in our program and a member of the program's working group despite most of them being from another state. Once the decision was confirmed to move to Auburn, Linda, and I (with some sorrow) sold our house in Colorado Springs and bought a house in Opelika (a small town practically connected to Auburn).

·n University and USA Team Handball have partnered to create
·-term Auburn Residency Program for both the Men's and
·n's National Teams in preparation for the 2016 Rio de Janeiro

We selected players with potential; young students usually from college (19–22 years of age) or just having finished their studies (21–25 years of age).

We worked at the beginning with less, but the group was complete with between sixteen and twenty-one players with periodic evaluations and changes if we found any better players in the tryouts.

Some of these athletes had some contact with handball, but most were first-time players. They often played basketball, American football, volleyball, baseball, and other sports.

It was a spectacular program for American handball with much better conditions than we had in New Jersey or Atlanta. We had a group at the beginning that varied between 14–18 players on the male team and 10–14 on the female team. After a few months both groups were full, although we continued with the policy of periodic tryouts.

During 2014, we adjusted our schedules. All that was missing was to start playing matches and having competitions regularly. We played several games with a men's team in Atlanta or had them come to Auburn. We established contacts with Canada, and throughout four years we exchanged visits to play tournaments.

Puerto Rico and Uruguay also visited our facilities so some of the official Qualifiers of the Pan American Federation were played first in Auburn and then in the Caribbean later.

In the spring of 2015, after several meetings and inspections by the Olympic Committee, the Auburn University Residency Program was declared an Olympic Handball Training Center. All those who in one way or another were involved in the program were very proud and satisfied with our accomplishment.

The daily work continued. The program in terms of training, medical care, testing, and even some research on the throwing motion and shoulders of some players was a success. But once again the money for competitions in America or Europe was a challenge. Harvey Schiller was elected as the new President of the Federation. He did not change things, and although his personal financial contribution and that of other managers meant we could extend the situation, he was not able to solve it at all. The program survived thanks to the sponsorship of a local medical care and insurance company which also provided medical services to our athletes. However, to continuously train without serious competition began to undermine the spirits and motivations of everyone. Work continued well on court level, but at the office level, roles and people shifted and opinions changed which led to a slowdown in how quickly some decisions were made.

At one point, I traveled to Madrid and decided, in coordination with the Federation, to schedule a meeting with Dr. Hassan Moustafa at the IHF offices in Basel. At that time, the IHF was very interested in the development of handball in large and populous countries such as China, India, and the USA.

We discussed at length the development and promotion of handball in the USA. He was very interested in presenting the plan we had been working on, so we agreed to organize a visit to Auburn so he could witness what was being done. The visit occurred and resulted in the announcement that the IHF would be willing to support and designate our program in Auburn as the first IHF Academy in America. At that time there were only two others in China. Ours would be the third in the world.

Visits by their members of the IHF followed one after another. And the meetings at the highest level between the three institutions, Auburn University, the IHF, and the USTHF continued as well, which the Olympic Committee later joined.

The idea in principle was very attractive. The idea would be to designate the site as a center of excellence focused on training players and curating the formation of a working group that would make up the national team. Also, the American players would have the opportunity to play in Europe. The group in Auburn formed a club and participated in regional tournaments (Ohio, North Carolina, Chicago) in addition to participating as a club in the National Championship. One year we finished in third. To train and hold competitions in Auburn allowed us to promote and increase the presence of handball in the media including TV.

Another very important section of the Academy is the work of training and certification of coaches and referees through courses, clinics, and symposia at the local, state, national and even the Pan American level. These courses would be directed by members of the Technical Commission of the IHF plus the coaches they deemed appropriate.

Another section of the academy would use the physiology and biomechanics laboratories to develop research tests for the creation of standards and scientific tests used for the selection of players. The three institutions signed a contract (the IHF, the USTHF, and Auburn University) and committed to working together.

We worked on it daily for three years (2015–2018). We elaborated on strategic plans to present to the Olympic Committee where we played friendly and official competitions in the USA and abroad (Canada, Chile, Mexico). All this while keeping in mind the financial issue as it was always a limiting factor. The USTHF never received sufficient funding to give players the necessary experience to be competitive. Each of the three Institutions (the IHF, the USTHF, Auburn University) expected from the other two, something more.

It was three great years as a coach. We created a new group of players. Some of them are in the group today of possible national team players: Alden, M. Lee, and Ty Reed.

We created a program recognized by Auburn University, the IHF, the USTHF, and the Olympic Committee. We had the IHF and Dr. Hassan willing to help but lacked the money to complete the project with high level international competition. We knew it was going to be difficult just as it was the other times in the last fifty years, but this time we had the ingredients. This time around we had the product and developed the necessary support to have done a much better job of marketing and fundraising.

I will not go into anything negative exposing and explaining this project in which we all put so much enthusiasm. Nevertheless, it was bigger than just not properly marketing and fundraising. It was always the same problem: the different agendas of different people, the lack of collaboration, and blaming others for their lack of effort. There was a need to get quick results, but those who wanted the quick results were not doing or letting others do what was necessary to get the results.

In addition to the work ongoing at Auburn, the plan was also to do regional work with juniors, along with the regional tournaments. We wanted to have several regional centers such as Auburn for young players to develop. We also wanted those working in the Residency Program for four years to play in Europe. A protocol with European clubs and Federations was implemented for when players went to Europe to ensure they were under our control and supervision.

We obtained the television signal of matches of the European Leagues, World Championships, and Olympics to broadcast monthly or weekly handball in the USA (through an agreement with the IHF and world and American television network). We improved the national club championship from the current form (one weekend, five matches) to a form similar to the sport festival where we had regional brackets rolling up to the finals. The goal was to apply the plans and wait for them to take effect.

As I said before we had three stimulating years (2015–2018), and with that came the feeling of knowing we were doing something worthwhile. In 2017, my wife Linda suddenly died. I continued to work a few more months, and in 2018 I retired and stepped away from all my duties at the USTHF.

I offer my greatest gratitude to all the people who I encountered throughout my fifty years in the sport: those who taught me as a player, those I taught as a coach, the directors who gave me the opportunity and the honor to do everything I did, and my family—especially my wife Linda, without whom I would not have been able to do even half of the things I did—I give great thanks and appreciation.

EUROPE–USA DIFFERENT OPINIONS IN TWO DIFFERENT WORLDS

On my many trips to Europe, I have had quite a few discussions with European coaches about handball in the USA and the difficulties we have finding players.

It is also difficult for them to understand the fact many players were past their adolescent years by the time they actually encountered handball whether it was on TV or playing it for the first time. Most coaches believe that if a person's first time playing handball is during their early '20s, they will more than likely not become great players. My goal for this book is to say that it is possible. It is definitely possible to make a competitive and valid player for a club or for a national team in a relatively short time—depending on the innate conditions the player possesses and the program to which we submit him/her. As long as the training and preparation is consistent, and his/her coaches can ensure periods of competition and evaluation, it can be done.

Why don't we start at younger ages? Handball is not included in the school sports school curricula and there are no competitions or clubs for boys and girls 13–19 years as there are in Europe. However, there are some clubs in certain regions of the country (such as areas that have European emigrants who played in their youth in Europe) with greater access to learn the game.

In the USA, elite sports are based on the work done in high school. Later, if the player excels, they are permitted to join the varsity teams of their university. After college, some players have the following options as far as their sports careers:

1. Play in the professional leagues if the sport has one (American football, baseball, hockey, NBA, etc.).
2. The second option is playing overseas. This often happens with those who want to extend their careers but are not selected by the American professional leagues.
3. Third option, since there are no second and third divisions like in Europe, they may not play on a team at all.

This is where we come in. There are many athletes who have finished four years of university and cannot enter the professional sports world. Nonetheless, several are still willing to dedicate a few more years to competitive sports and are motivated by the possibility of participating in an Olympiad. They would not make the Olympic basketball team, but if a door to Olympism opens and they are willing to spend 2–4 years or more to give it a try they just might. Being an Olympian in the USA is a great honor.

The Olympic world in the USA is different from the rest of the world. There are no subsidies or sponsorships, or public money at the municipal, state, or federal level. There is no ministry of sports or a superior council of sport. All the money from the Olympic Committee to the Federations, clubs, and individually has to be obtained through private donations, fundraising, and sponsorships. I believe it takes special motivation to provoke an athletes' desire to become an Olympian as it comes with great sacrifice and life changing decisions.

With the reality of school sports in the USA, I would like to reinforce the idea that it is possible to attain competitive players at the international level by providing examples of those who were in the same position and have succeeded. There are opportunities for America's best athletes to play in Europe and many have played in the first, second, or third Bundesliga division.

I will refer only to the players with whom I had a direct relationship, worked with me for a while, and later became players under the discipline of clubs in the European Leagues. Their careers took place during the time I worked for the American Federation in 1979 to 1987—preparing for the 1984 Olympiad in Los Angeles—and the 1987 Pan American Games in Indianapolis—when we qualified for the Seoul 1988 Olympiad.

Steve Goss: Goss was one of our best players. He played for a year at Club Atlético de Madrid and did not continue because he had to finish his veterinary studies, which were already postponed after three years of work in New Jersey prior to the Los Angeles '84 Olympics. Steve was perhaps the most cross-functional player (defense and attack) we had on the team. He came from a club in California and joined the Residential Program that we established in New Jersey from the beginning (July 1981).

Peter Lash: Our powerful scorer from the left side had offers from teams in Switzerland and Germany. He rejected because as a graduate of the West Point Military Academy, he had to complete five years of service after his time on the national and Olympic team ended.

Joe Story: He played for two years at Atlético Madrid prior to Los Angeles '84, where he was the undisputed starter on the left wing.

Bill Kessler: He played for one year at Caja Madrid.

Bob Djokovich: Center back and Team Captain. Was a great organizer and scorer as he demonstrated with his performance in the World Championship in Italy in 1987. He surprised us and created trends with his trick-filled passes.

Rod Oshita and Tom Schneeberger, Jimmy Buehning could have played perfectly on European teams.

Considering the collective aspect of what we achieved as a team at the end of the program, we can declare the following: July 1981 to July 1984 (Los Angeles), were three years of full dedication. The following is a list of results from the Olympic competition.

GERMANY 21 – USA 19	SWEDEN 21 – USA 18
DENMARK 19 – USA 16	SPAIN 17 – USA 16
KOREA 22 – USA 22	USA 24 – JAPAN 16

From 1984 to 1987, there was no Residency Program and daily training. We had more European components with periodic training and the rest of the time they worked in clubs.

In the 1987 Pan American Games in Indianapolis, we were champions. We won in the final against Cuba which meant the Qualification for the Seoul 1988 Olympiad.

They were good players and a good team logically at continental level. I'm not saying they were the best, but considering the time frame, they did an exceptionally good job.

$$3 \text{ years} + 3 \text{ years} = 6 \text{ years}$$

The next generation that worked to prepare for the Atlanta Olympics also had players who played internationally.

Derick Heath played in Sweden for several years and was very impressive with his jumping ability and his shooting from 10–11 meters.

Dave DeGraaf didn't play internationally, but he was one of the best defenders I've seen in my entire career.

We could increase the men's list, but I want to emphasize a player from international women's handball who played in the '80s and early '90s. Her name is **Sam Jones.** She was without a doubt the best player on the USA team in Los Angeles '84 and after the Olympiad she went to play for Hypo Bank, Austria, and

Bayer Leverkusen in Germany—top club teams at that time. She also participated in the Seoul Olympics '88. She became one of the best players in the world. It is with great honor for me to share how and when Sam Jones started playing handball.

In the fall of 1981, Professor Wayne Edwards received positive information from the University at North Carolina regarding a college basketball player who was about to graduate.

I hosted a tryout in New Jersey (where the team was training) with Sam and two judo athletes. The three girls trained in the gym for two sessions on a Saturday and one on Sunday. Sam's innate abilities were out of the ordinary in all the passing exercises, receptions, steps, and jumps.

Collectively, she possessed skills in alternating shots from different angles of the goal coupled with a natural ease as if she had done it all her life. She had great ease of defensive movement. In a word, one of the best discoveries in all the time I worked in the USA.

At the end of the three sessions, I meet with Sam and told her, "Sam, in a week we are going to Germany to play some games and we would like you to come with us as a new member of the team, and at the same time you can see and live handball and the reality of the national team."

Sam decided to come with us, and within almost ten days of knowing the sport, she debuted with the team and participated in the matches.

We returned from Europe, and I invited her to join the group in Lake Placid where the team had lived and trained. She replied after a few days informing me she could not go. Her family did not allow it. Her sister explained that they were not very convinced that it was the best thing for Sam. With great regret on my part, she did not accept the invitation.

As I said before, all this happened in the fall of 1981. The Women's Team went to the Lake Placid Olympic Center, and the Men's team continued in New Jersey. We continued our work and in July 1982, Sam became a part of the Eastern Regional Team at the sports festival.

At the end of the National Sports Festival, Sam told me her family had changed their minds and allowed her to join the team. This was great news for handball USA. Sam Jones joined the training group at Lake Placid around September 1982.

In July 1984, she was one of the best players on the national team and the Olympic tournament. From that platform she jumped to two of the best European women's clubs where she played for several years and participated again at the Seoul Olympiad.

Yes, it is possible to make a good player, even if she starts her career in handball at 22–23 years old.

HOW DO WE DO IT?

The first thing we need to do is find the players by way of : The national coaches, our assistants, and coaches of clubs. Tournaments are organized two or three times a year. For example, the National Championship of Universities and the National Open Championship—each on separate dates, where the best clubs in the country participate.

Years ago, we had the National Sports Festival in which the country was divided into four regional teams. All the best players were there so we were able to identify new talent as well as players we knew.

Every 2–3 months the Federation organized tryouts when we were in New Jersey from 1981 to 1984. I already mentioned that every six months (July and

December), we evaluated all twenty-one players and sometimes they would be sent home or new players added.

These tryouts were advertised through clubs, sometimes Federation publications, local newspapers, radio, etc. With the arrival of the internet, information was passed along via the Federation website and often just by word of mouth throughout the handball community. Anyone could participate. If I found someone who was better or thought they might be better in the future than one of the twenty-one players who were already with us, I would add them to the group.

HOW DO WE SELECT THEM?

The format of a tryout is as follows:

The athlete has to fill out a series of forms where he/she must provide their resume and a simple medical record. Each athlete has to become a member of the Federation to benefit from the health insurance that the Federation provides to all its members and sign a letter exempting the Federation from liability in case of injury.

They appear in the gym, and we have a meeting in which they are informed of all the legal issues discussed above. In addition to this, we discuss the options and opportunities that can be taken advantage of if they are selected for the national team.

The tryout consists of three sessions: Saturday morning, Saturday afternoon, and Sunday morning. I do not do physical tests. Years ago, they were done but now the physical part was evaluated with the observation and development of the player during the three sessions.

First session:
- The first session is dedicated mainly to attack and defense technique:
  - Pass–reception, step cycle, dynamic reception and pass shooting trajectories, location in the goal, different shooting angles—which leads to shots from different positions. Passes and receptions in support and jump. Reception from the left, step cycle, pass to the right, the same but pass to the left. Changes of direction and feints, strong points, and weak points.

- Defensive movements front and back, laterals, basic defensive position, contact technique 1:1. Work against the ball, interceptions, deterrence, and blocks.

- Defensive movements front and back, laterals, basic defensive position, contact technique 1:1. Work against the ball, interceptions, deterrence, and blocks.

Exercises must be combined with all these concepts with minimum explanation and maximum time dedicated to the practical execution of the technical elements presented. This will last a total of two hours and half an hour for the final part with counterattack exercises (long and short passes).

Second session:
- The first part is thirty minutes like in the morning and ninety more applied to 2:2, 3:3 and 4:4. The last 20–30 minutes are 6:6 matches.

Third session:
- Sunday morning, two hours dedicated to twenty-minute matches with different groups, varying teams, and playing positions.

What do we look for when we observe all these exercises? What qualities do we want to see in athletes?

- We want to see natural abilities that cannot be significantly improved in training—natural power, speed, and jumping ability.
- Agility in defensive movements, forward, backward, lateral.

From here we evaluate all the elements of the individual technique in attack and defense. The exercises we use demonstrate whether a player can execute and master these elements.

Some might ask, "If you've never played, how are you going to do all this?" Here comes the most important thing. The one who can't do it doesn't interest me; we look for the one who can do it or the one who makes the fewest mistakes, and the one who understands the meaning and objectives when executing the exercises. We identify athletes who continue to concentrate and immediately overcome mistakes and remain poised and positive. These are the individuals who can be useful to us.

At the beginning of the first session, I did not give instructions on how to use the arm to throw. Yes, I explained the steps and their relationship in time with the arm, but from there I wanted to see who could throw innately and who couldn't. In my experience after dozens of tryouts, there are people who know how to throw and people who have to be taught to throw. Throwing is a natural skill like running. There are people who know how to run and people who have to be taught to run.

In both cases, with training and learning, you improve and master these skills. Keep in mind we have limited time if we want to become Olympians in two years. Second, there are other things you cannot do if you cannot shoot which adds more delay and difficulty. And third point regarding if we have to teach a player to throw if he does not have the natural movement to do so, the player will need to rebuild coordination, nerves, and muscle synchronization of the arm. Especially the shoulder which will produce cases of discomfort (stiffness) and at worst, muscle pain and injury, tendonitis, etc. which will require treatment and rest. You have to be very good at many other things to make up for this shortcoming.

To continue with throwing the (pass or shot on goal) training, there are peculiarities more clearly presented in the USA than in Europe.

Most of the players were former basketball players, but sometimes we selected people from football or baseball. There were specific traits in each of them that I thought could aid in shot training. The basketball player always has the ball in front of his body, and never passes the line from his shoulders except when he passes with two hands above his head. The rest of the passes and throws are with two or one hand, but always in front of the shoulders.

Former players have difficulty carrying the throwing arm with the ball back to have more power to launch. When they are able to find their rhythm, the coach will need to train them on the speed at which they do it. They are slower at throwing than the bad guy's horse in Westerns. You have to laugh from time to time.

American football players usually advance the coordinated movement of the elbow before aligning with the shoulder as they will have consequent loss of power and speed of the ball in addition to not having the hand behind the ball at the time of throw. In football it is necessary that the hand is on the side of the ball to be able to give the spin to the ball so that it "flies" and rotates horizontally.

In baseball the difference is the ball is much smaller and practically becomes an extension of the wrist and fingers. The different throws depend in part on the way the fingers catch the ball, sometimes even involving the nails.

In handball, the opening of the hand to hold the ball greatly limits the movements of the wrist. Hence there can be a big difference when you see the same person throwing our ball and throwing the ball for a different sport with the same arm at such different speeds.

The next difficulty new players will face in handball is decision making. Decision making is part of every sport but building a foundation and understanding the objectives in handball is key to achieving success. As an example, defending the goal vs intercept the pass.

Decision making consists of:

- Perception
- Evaluation
- Execution

If I am planning an attack and I do not have the ball, I have to observe where the ball is, where my opponent is, if they pass me the ball, and *where* I must attack so that the defense has more difficulty. If I make a move too soon and I get too close to the defender they might intercept the ball. In this case, I have challenged my teammate with the ball with the risk of error on his part, and I have also wasted a possibility of me being open to receive the pass.

When we transfer this to training and the objectives of the exercises, we find the following:

- Players who wait to receive the ball often start attacking too late.
- Players who observe what opponents, teammates, etc. are going to do but move too soon, and cannot receive the ball.
- Players who receive the ball with good passing time but then make a poor decision, for example, deciding in advance to shoot against two defenders when the adjacent teammate is wide open.

I found that Sam Jones learned fairly quickly. Other players, however, needed more time to learn this skill.

Decision making is also important in terms of connecting with teammates to advance down the court. If the team works well together there can be a feeling of success when in the previous attack the player manages to penetrate between two defenders. And before the split jump by the goalkeeper, the attacker throws between his legs to score.

Other aspects we look for include:

- Height, speed, power, jumping, throwing speed, tactical intelligence in decision making, tactical intelligence in defense, bravery, and courage in defensive contacts 1:1 and the same in blocking shots.

- Humility, attitude, and attention all the time. Intensity with self-control.
- Generosity and companionship with unfamiliar peers.

There is another bad habit these adult players have, especially basketball players. It is to dribble as soon as they receive the ball. I think that's because in basketball only two steps are allowed, and handball has three. By doing this we lose the first cycle of steps. Dribbling instead of using three steps and finding a shooting position form is totally harmless; therefore, we do not attract the attention of the defender. To lose the concept of fixing the defender is to lose a very important part of the fundamentals of the attack.

Therefore, what we want to see is:
- Receive the ball while moving
- Execute the first cycle of steps (in zone to shoot or get in throwing position)
- Dribble and take a second cycle of steps (with change, of direction) and complete the shot or pass

Any attack that does not end at least in fixing or drawing the defender is not worth anything. It is simply a transfer of the ball from one attacker to the next.

These are a few things to look out for when working with athletes from different sports.

Thus far, I've talked about the difficulties and challenges the players encounter when starting handball so late, but there is a great advantage that can balance this out.

European youth players and juniors have to go through the test of an important competition where there will be different levels of play with stronger and more expert opponents, and the pressure of the public (2,000 people) in an International Junior Championship.

A twenty-two-year-old basketball player, a graduate of X university which is a good basketball program has been playing important games in front of 16,000 spectators sometimes at home and sometimes in away settings with very passionate fans. Stage fright, responsibility, work habits, routines and game preparation protocols are things they might not need to learn if they have already had these experiences. Also, the American player has a special motivation to be an Olympian and you are giving him that opportunity. You have given him a shirt that says "USA." He is lined up in a row and listening to the national anthem.

In the trips we made to Europe to play matches, we played against different categories of teams: Bundesliga, Asobal of Spain, tournaments in Norway with Denmark and Russia, etc. For this older athlete, the German Second Division Team is the same as the Danish National Team in Norway (I do not say the Russian National Team because maybe it is a little more special). It can be a great advantage—an athlete who is mature, educated, intelligent, and accustomed to discipline and hard work. This can be very valuable to the team and the athlete may receive more respect from his team and coaches even though he may not have the same technical skill.

But you still must teach that athlete those technical skills. Even if the athlete is 1.98 m tall with a very good jump, he must learn jumpshots from 11 m with precision and two or three locations, great shot blocking and forceful 1:1 contacts. These skills are critical.

Older athletes also understand the counter attack and the phases of the game. Yes, you select that twenty-two-year-old athlete who impressed you as he took the three steps and threw. Now he is in front of the team in Norway, waiting for you to say what he has to do to score against the Norwegians.

This reminds me of the idea I came up with to defend Vasilyev, left back of Russia. Vasilyev will always come to you. With his steps, he wants to fake you. Left, right to go to the center, anticipate, jump, shoot. Close your left side, and do not let him go to the center. If he is going to a weak point, be attentive that he does not always do it. But if he does it to you, that goal is on me, the coach.

It is critical to perfect the exercise of passing from side to side and the changing of sides moving backwards without losing sight of the game. Also, the attack at the right time with the right trajectory, receiving in 11 m and passing in 9 m, allowing peripheral vision to make us see what is happening on the other side of the court and thus adapting the attack to the right timing.

Attack at the right time means to receive the ball at 11 m while moving. Then observe what happens in front and in the goal. Have the throwing arm prepared in the second step and in the third, (normally with the opposite leg of the throwing arm) and shoot or if you cannot finish, pass to the other side.

This exercise is a basic part of my training. The warm-ups are simple and progressively we add difficulty, increasing the speed of execution in the movement and the handling of the ball from the moment it is received to the moment of release in the pass-shoot phase. On defense, we want defenders in the line of pass or hindering the handling of the ball, even touching or fouling. Visual stimuli in the goal means different types of passes or technical action, location of the shot, etc.

There is another circumstance I would like to point out and it has to do with the fact that in handball we have two levels of defensive action. On the one hand, there is the plane of defenders distributed in the system (6–0, 3-2-1, etc.). The finisher of the attack has to overcome the defender in penetration or jumping, and surpass him in support using a 2:2 in crossing or in dynamic blocking in 8 m. All this is going to require a good decision, intensity, and quick reflexes and decisions. Now sometimes we did all this and surpassed the defender, but we still had to overcome the goalkeeper's defense.

In basketball, on the other hand, we seek to overcome the defender with the technical moves and the necessary skill that in most cases, will need maximum intensity and effort. Once the defense has been overcome, the basket does not move and the attacker, after the intense effort against the defender, has then "relaxed" and shoots with skill and touch. There is no goalkeeper.

Sometimes I have noticed in new players, involuntary habits of working hard and concentrating against the defender. And almost always looking for the skill to beat the defender but then the shot is weak or easily blocked.

My advice in these cases is not to make "a world" out of all this. The two planes of defensive action demand attackers to always throw hard and lose that habit of lowering the intensity once the player has exceeded the defender.

In actuality, this point of the two defensive planes in handball, is a bit delicate and not as simple as I have explained. It requires time and work to master it. There is a lot of strategy in the collaboration of the defense/goalkeeper—and it presents more difficulty for the attackers. Nonetheless, it is not my intention to go into those issues, but if I say that it exists, the new players have to learn to dominate double difficulty, so when that occurs, it will happen reflexively without thinking about it. If you have to think too long about it, it will be too late.

Having said that, coaches have to be careful not to create confusion and frustration in the new players. It is one more part of their learning (and not the development of the atomic bomb)—that they will figure out.

HOW WE TEACH THEM.

I have never considered myself an expert in methodology. I was always a trainer whose methods were more focused on the practical part than the theoretical. Likewise, I have always liked planning; I have always had a plan no matter what activity I was doing.

With the passage of time and perhaps influenced by the fact that I never trained with younger boys or girls, I was increasingly taking more pleasure in the practical part of work. What I found to be extremely important and necessary for the development of these players was to master the essential skills to be a competitive handball player as soon as possible. Let's not waste time or useless energy listening to concepts and ideas that you will never or almost never have to use. These theoretical ideas may be important for the coach to correctly present at some point. Yet, it is essential to choose the exercises and training that each player in particular needs and not to spend his time and energies on other concepts. That's what measures the quality and success of the coach.

I hope it has become clear—especially at the beginning of my career—that I was a practical coach. With experience and daily work brings new goals, opening new paths that force you to adapt.

My relationship with Professor Luis Carlos Torrescusa was decisive for me. The work and ideas he captured in the book the Spanish Federation published, together with the Olympic Committee in 1992, were and continue to be the compass that marks my course in terms of methodology and the different stages of learning.

He increased my perspective and managed to synthesize and compress all those ideas and greatly facilitated my teaching with the players. Those ideas hovered in my head without knowing how they would land, but it was essential that they did. Theoretical and difficult for players to digest, has to become something simple and understandable for everyone, which is our main task as coaches. We must simplify, prioritize, and choose what is really important and necessary to master, and discard what is less important.

All this was also possible with the help of Professor Manuel Laguna and specifically the work he did with me in the time we worked together in Portugal.

I will try to synthesize as much as possible the methodology we applied based on the ideas of these two experts.

In Spain we subdivide the learning periods into:

GLOBAL LEARNING	(10–11 years)	YOUTH
SPECIFIC INITIATION	(12–13–14 years)	CHILDREN
SPECIFIC LEARNING	(15–16 years)	CADETS
IMPROVEMENT	(17–18–19 years)	CADETS

Just looking at the ages we know there is something different about the players. Some are 13–15 years old and maybe others 18-19. There are many things we can and must teach a youth player that an older player doesn't need.

TEACHING

1. We dispense with the global learning phase, eliminating pre-sports games and simplified games, but maintaining the acquisition of fundamental techniques and the introduction to the formation of decision schemes.
2. We start the coaching of adult players by turning ourselves totally into the phases of specific learning and improvement.

We focus on:
1. Teaching the real game.
2. Selecting positions the players are best suited for.
3. Working the four phases of the game:
   - Defense
   - Counterattack

- Organized attack game
- Defensive withdrawal

4. Teaching from the first day, the organization and the tempo of the game
5. Reducing and understanding spaces.
6. Using technical and tactical elements in positions.
7. Using tactical procedures.
8. Using zone defenses—deep play in attack (penetrations and playing with pivot).

In the improvement phase:
1. The physical preparation acquires a great emphasis in the adult ages that are already developed, which can be an advantage of starting with older athletes.
2. Parallel development of technical-tactical conditions and skills.
3. Maximum specialization in the position and search for efficiency.
4. Learning situations similar to the real game.
5. Improvement and mastery of the technical aspects.

At this point I would like to emphasize two things:

- Depending on each country and each school or culture of basketball, there are always certain nuances that create differences from one type of player to another. For example, the Nordics (Sweden, Denmark) have an exceptional passing quality and devote much of their learning time to the technique of passing. Several years later the result and the degree of accuracy that leads to success can be clearly seen despite the possible predictability on the part of the defender.
- On the other hand, in Spain, more work is done, and more time is devoted to individual tactics than to technique. Our players are not so predictable and have more variety and more ability to surprise. Logically that is accompanied by more inaccuracy and more possibility of error.

In my opinion, the two tendencies should reinforce what they already have and work to improve what they do not.

Another point I would like to make applies to defense. In most European schools, they teach defense starting with open defenses and 1:1 or man-to-man to dominate and control your opponent with little help. Then they gradually learn the zone defenses (6–0, 5-1, 3- 2-1, etc.).

It is better to work and teach the zone defenses, gradually open the spaces, and extend the zone defense until you reach 3–3 or even individual defense in 12–13 m.

It is interesting since basketball players are perfectly accustomed to defending 1:1 in large spaces and understand perfectly and "read" the game of individual defense.

Perhaps because of this and the fact they need to better understand defensive strategies and individual tasks for handball is why they prefer to start dominating opponents and spaces by using more help and learning the individual tasks of different systems. They open up more and more and begin to instinctively read the game. Let them dig up their basketball habits that we must not forget they already have inside.

My training goes directly to the root of the matter. New players need to know and practice the skills, strategies, and movements the rules allow both in defense and attack (1:1).

Players have to know the possible connections they can make with another player (2:2) or with collective tactical procedures:

ATTACK = Successive penetrations – Crosses – Pass and go – Screens

DEFENSE = Assists (helping) – Change of opponent – Slippage – Counter lock

This is our roadmap in the training plans to which more tasks will be added until completing the 6:6 work in games.

We are going to summarize all the concepts we have mentioned so far about the learning process—philosophy that we apply in detecting talent.

We look for innate skills that cannot be improved with training. and good athletes who are tall with good jumping ability and know how to throw and make decisions quickly.

"AMERICAN WAY" METHODOLOGY

We dispense with the global stage of learning and go straight to specific learning.

ATTACK

1. Individual technique–individual tactics.
2. Ability to transport the ball (receptions, passes, dribbles).
3. Ability to create shooting situations.
4. Shot quality.

The player in attack has to be dangerous.

- He has to "read" the game to take advantage of the opportunities that others create.
- He must be clear about the concept of continuity, which means he can pass laterally on both sides—pass deep to pivot or behind to another coming across.
- He must master collective tactical procedures 2:2.
- He must make successive penetrations—attacking the spaces between two or attacking the odd defender.
- He must make crosses and pass and go.
- He must block static in 6 m or dynamic in 9 m.

DEFENSE

The player in defense has to assimilate and master the factors of individual tactics that will help him in marking attackers.

- Location — passing line or shooting line
- Distance — which depends on the position of the opponent or the situation of the ball
- Orientation — opponent and ball

- Technical position — correct 1:1 contact

Then the player must take on all defensive tasks and adapt to the different movements of the opposition. Work against the opponent, work against the ball. Master defensive tactical procedures. Help and prevent the 1:2 before it occurs. Change opponents when necessary. Defend the pass and go. Counter-blockades. An important trend applied by the defense: anticipation = dissuasion = variety of formations.

Given this, the attack may use dynamic swaps. Expand spaces with the ball for another. Create spaces unmarked without the ball. Use perpendicular situations (frontal attack and lateral blocking) as well as long blocks.

There are also times and moments of the attack that the player must understand and initiate the attack group (2–3–4 players). And also decision making (when to continue the attack, when the offense has an advantage). If it is not a good opportunity, keep possession of the ball, reorganize, but be mindful of passive play.

PRACTICAL PART

The workouts and exercises were intended to be simple with a lot of information, including having a meeting with the new players outside the training time to explain the objectives and skills that would be worked on in training.

During training you have to pay special attention to new players to make sure they follow instructions and stick to them as closely as possible, as well as observe how they relate to the rest of the team.

Weekly Microcycle:
- Monday–Friday = train every day in the afternoon 7:00 p.m.–9:00 p.m. We alternate giving one day priority to attack and another to defense.
- Monday–Wednesday–Friday = attack
- Tuesday–Thursday = defense-counter
- Saturday and Sunday = break unless there is a match or tournament. Also, some Saturday mornings we would do conditioning outside the gym, if there was no game.

- Monday–Wednesday–Friday = weight training with weights in the mornings (8:30 a.m.–10:00 a.m.) before classes or jobs.

Depending on the microcycles and mesocycles, we changed the days we practiced attack or defense. The distribution of work times lines in training continued depending on whether it was training with attack or defense objectives.

The methodology applied toward practical exercises developed in the gym were mostly the same exercises and sessions used in Spain in the different learning periods. There were two specific blocks of exercises and tasks to be carried out in the practical sessions:

1. Those relating to the improvement of perception and decision making belong to the practical part of the presentation created by Prof. Manuel Laguna at the IHF Symposium in Lisbon 2003.
2. Those relating to the practical sessions which were recommended and subsequently carried out in the teen/cadet trainings of the Talent Detection Program and base handball which took place in the Spanish Federation.

Many of the sessions and exercises we did with the players were based on and followed the guidelines of these two great blocks of work. Alternating and planning daily and weekly the time we dedicate to the work of:

$$1:1 - 2:2 - 3:3 - 4:4 = 6:6$$

You all know how important it is to master and to train all these parts of attack and defense.

In my plans I like to relate the 1:1 with the 3:3 and the 2:2 with the 4:4. The tactical procedures used in each of them have more similarities, and we put the player in situations and experiences of learning from the beginning to develop connection.

1:1 and 3:3 are the most used training methods. They include successive penetrations and crosses. The 2:2 and 4:4 are of course usable, but the fourth player connects the 2:2 in amplitude. The game in two lines with any player entering pivot allows deep play and static blocks in 6 m, or dynamic play between lines, or in 9 m, or the pass and go.

The connection and the step from 4:4 to 6:6 is almost obvious, and I am going to say that if we have a good 4:4 we will have a good 6:6. I am very clear if we have a bad 4:4, we surely will not have a good 6:6.

The series of practical works I propose go directly to the center of the issue when we talk about improvement of recognition and decision making, and the sessions are planned to work and alternate the tasks for the improvement and practice of the tactical procedures in attack and defense.

Playbook

OBJETIVO GENERAL

INTRODUCCIÓN DE CONCEPTOS BÁSICOS TÉCNICO-TÁCTICOS DE ATAQUE Y DEFENSA

PROPÓSITO ESPECÍFICO

TAREAS	DESCRIPCIÓN

1. Calefacción:
- CARRERAS, ROTACIONES, ESTIRAMIENTOS
- TRABAJA CON FUERZA

2. Pase yrecepción

- un balón con el pie, otro con la mano

- uno defiende al otro, los dos driblan el balón.

3. Juego de "10 pases"

4. Calentamiento delportero

Parte principal

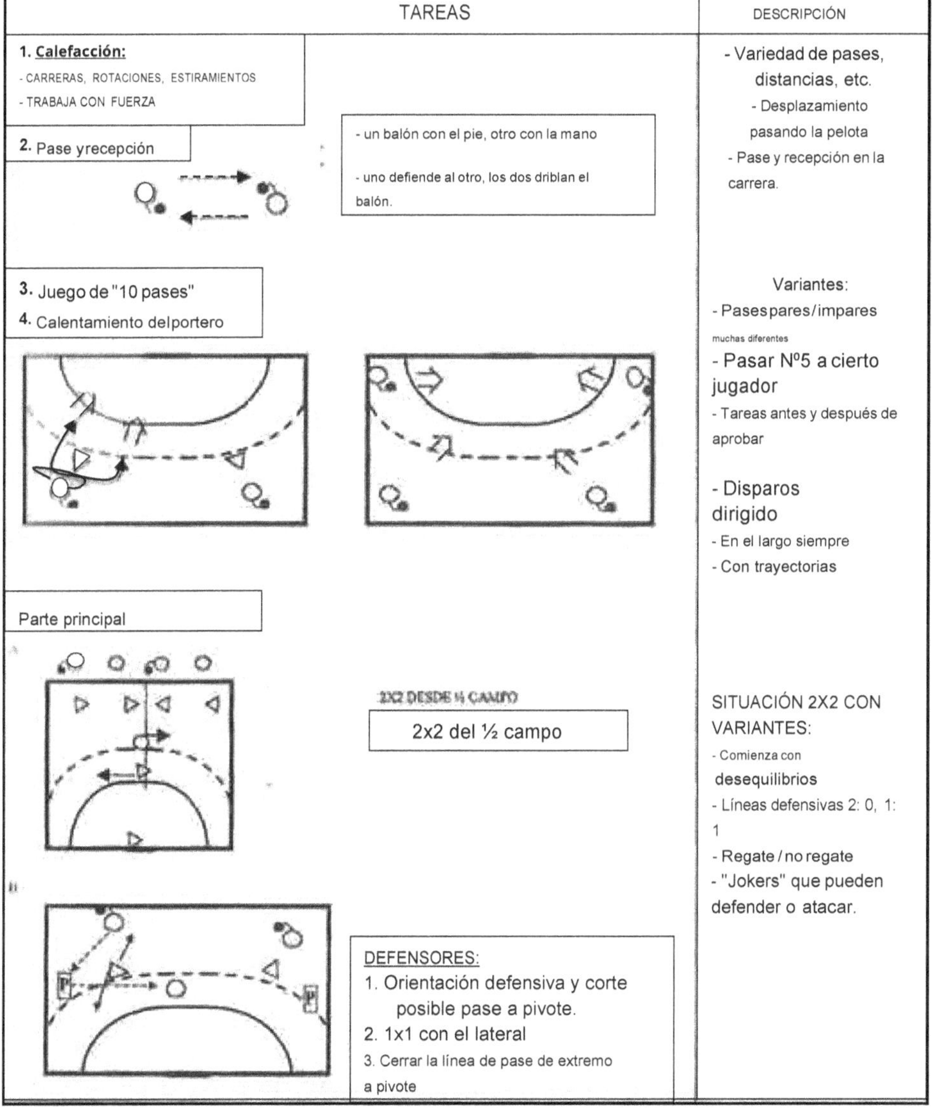

2x2 del ½ campo

DEFENSORES:
1. Orientación defensiva y corte posible pase a pivote.
2. 1x1 con el lateral
3. Cerrar la línea de pase de extremo a pivote

Descripción:

- Variedad de pases, distancias, etc.
- Desplazamiento pasando la pelota
- Pase y recepción en la carrera.

Variantes:
- Pasespares/impares
muchas diferentes
- Pasar Nº5 a cierto jugador
- Tareas antes y después de aprobar

- Disparos dirigido
- En el largo siempre
- Con trayectorias

SITUACIÓN 2X2 CON VARIANTES:
- Comienza con desequilibrios
- Líneas defensivas 2: 0, 1: 1
- Regate / no regate
- "Jokers" que pueden defender o atacar.

TAREAS	DESCRIPCIÓN

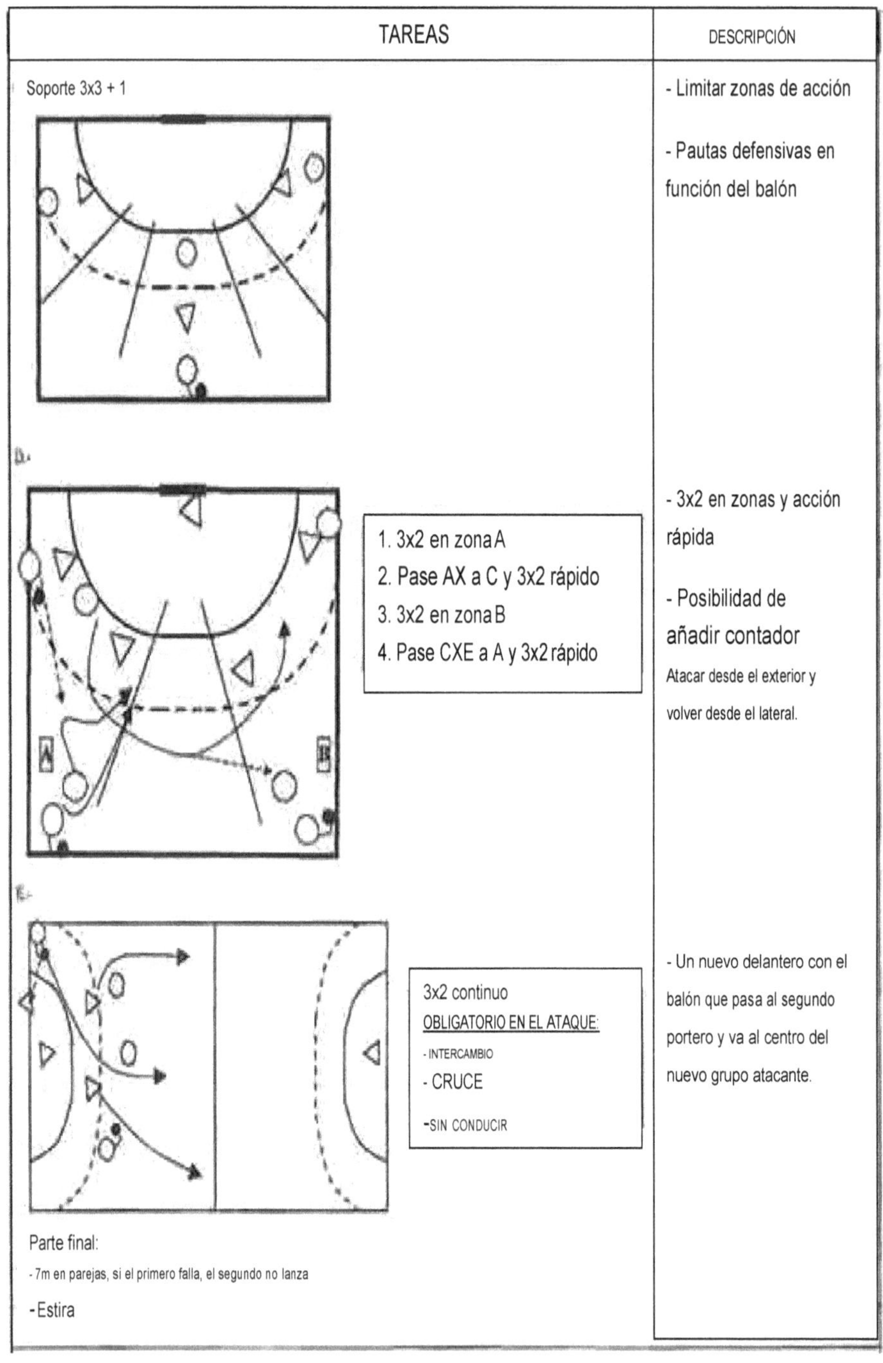

DESCRIPCIÓN

- Limitar zonas de acción

- Pautas defensivas en función del balón

- 3x2 en zonas y acción rápida

- Posibilidad de añadir contador

Atacar desde el exterior y volver desde el lateral.

- Un nuevo delantero con el balón que pasa al segundo portero y va al centro del nuevo grupo atacante.

Parte final:

- 7m en parejas, si el primero falla, el segundo no lanza

- Estira

OBJETIVO GENERAL

TEC-TAT DEFENSIVO INDIVIDUAL

PROPÓSITO ESPECÍFICO

- Posiciones base, compensaciones, orientaciones, línea de paso, marcado y control del oponente, bloques

1. Calefacción: - desplazamientos/estiramientos libres
                 - juegos

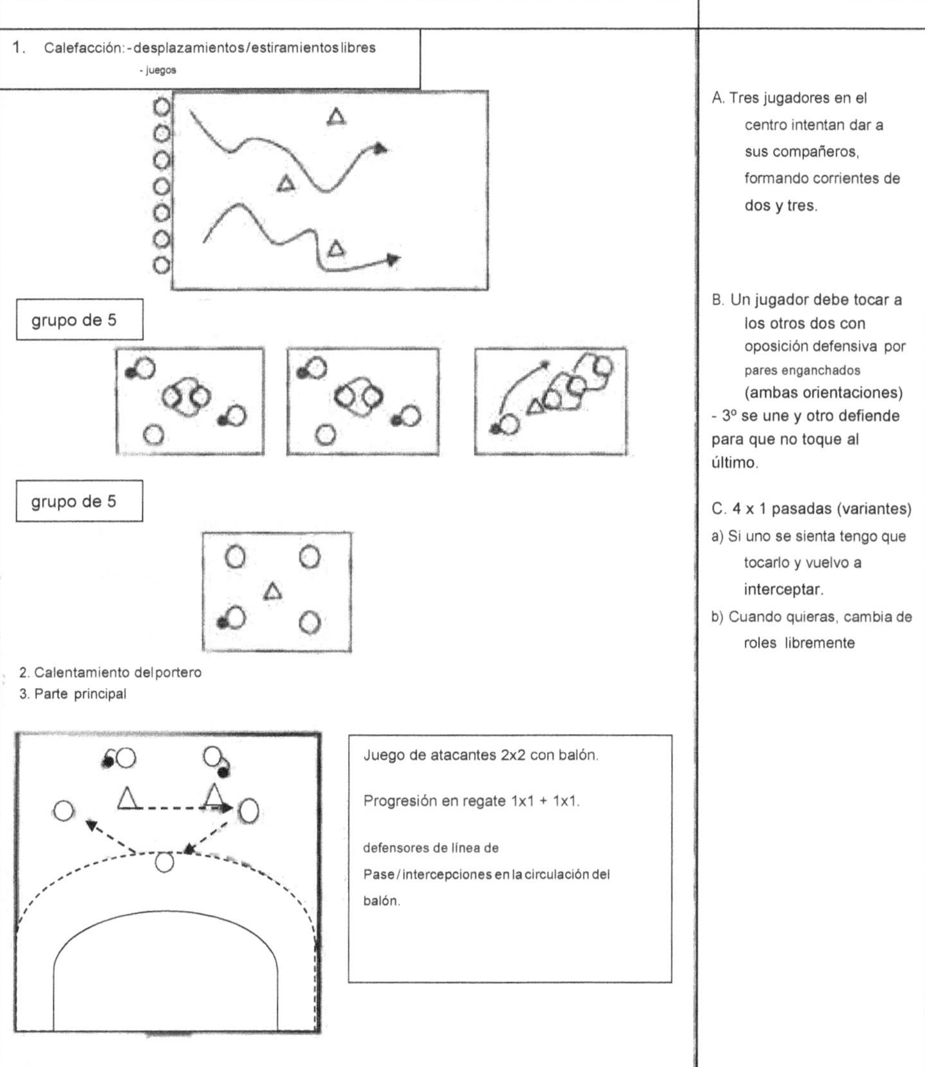

grupo de 5

grupo de 5

2. Calentamiento del portero
3. Parte principal

A. Tres jugadores en el centro intentan dar a sus compañeros, formando corrientes de dos y tres.

B. Un jugador debe tocar a los otros dos con oposición defensiva por pares enganchados (ambas orientaciones)
- 3º se une y otro defiende para que no toque al último.

C. 4 x 1 pasadas (variantes)
a) Si uno se sienta tengo que tocarlo y vuelvo a interceptar.
b) Cuando quieras, cambia de roles libremente

TAREAS	DESCRIPCIÓN

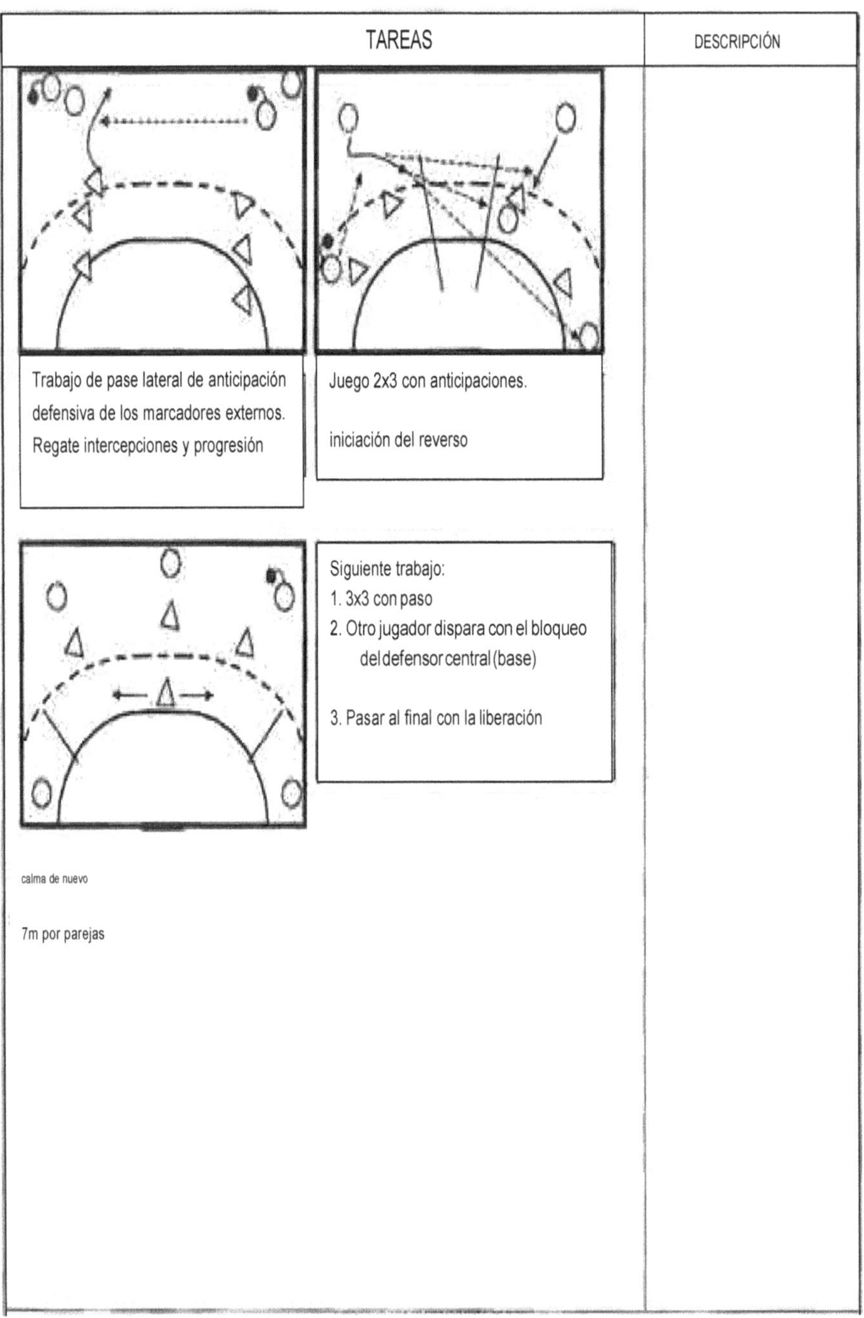

Trabajo de pase lateral de anticipación defensiva de los marcadores externos. Regate intercepciones y progresión

Juego 2x3 con anticipaciones.

iniciación del reverso

Siguiente trabajo:
1. 3x3 con paso
2. Otro jugador dispara con el bloqueo del defensor central (base)

3. Pasar al final con la liberación

calma de nuevo

7m por parejas

OBJETIVO GENERAL

PRINCIPIOS BÁSICOS DE CONTRA-ATAQUE

PROPÓSITO ESPECÍFICO

- Definir espacios de acción

TAREAS	DESCRIPCIÓN
Calefacción	

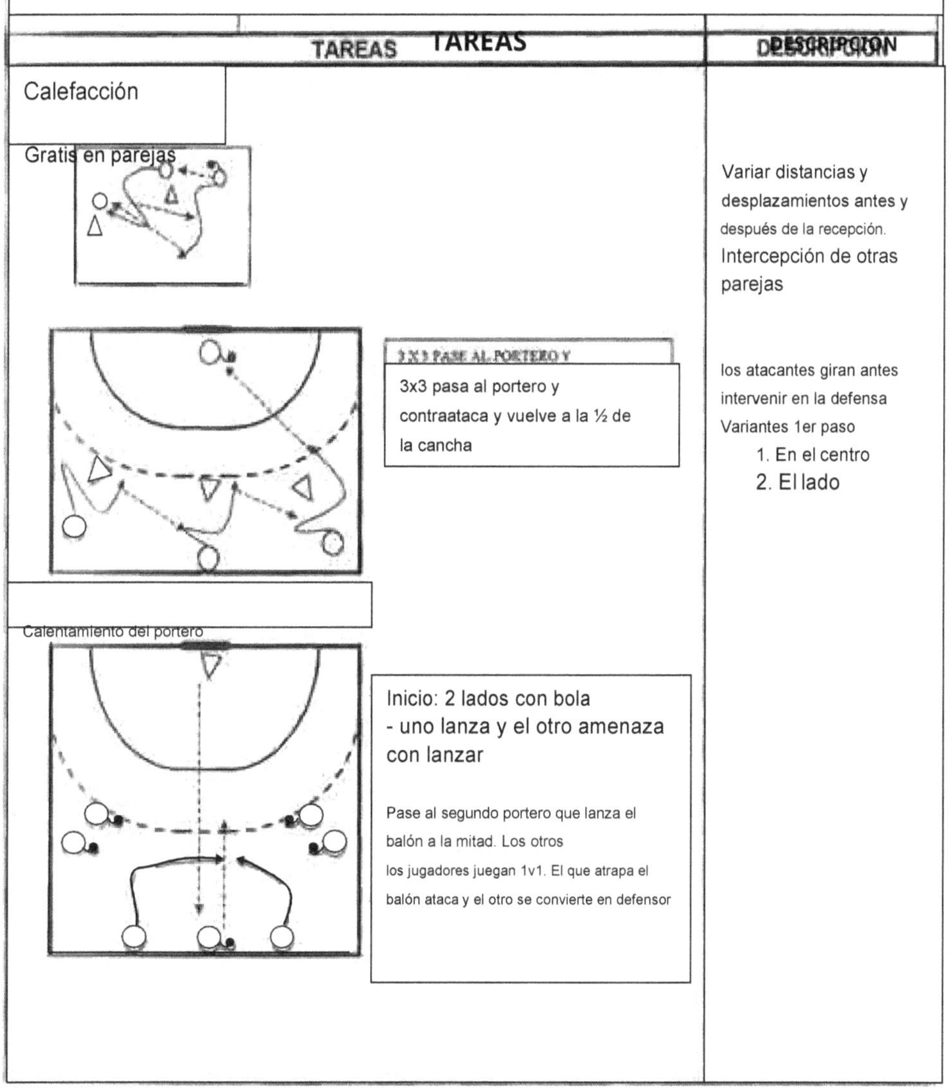

Variar distancias y desplazamientos antes y después de la recepción.
Intercepción de otras parejas

los atacantes giran antes intervenir en la defensa
Variantes 1er paso
1. En el centro
2. El lado

Inicio: 2 lados con bola
- uno lanza y el otro amenaza con lanzar

Pase al segundo portero que lanza el balón a la mitad. Los otros
los jugadores juegan 1v1. El que atrapa el balón ataca y el otro se convierte en defensor

TAREAS	DESCRIPCIÓN

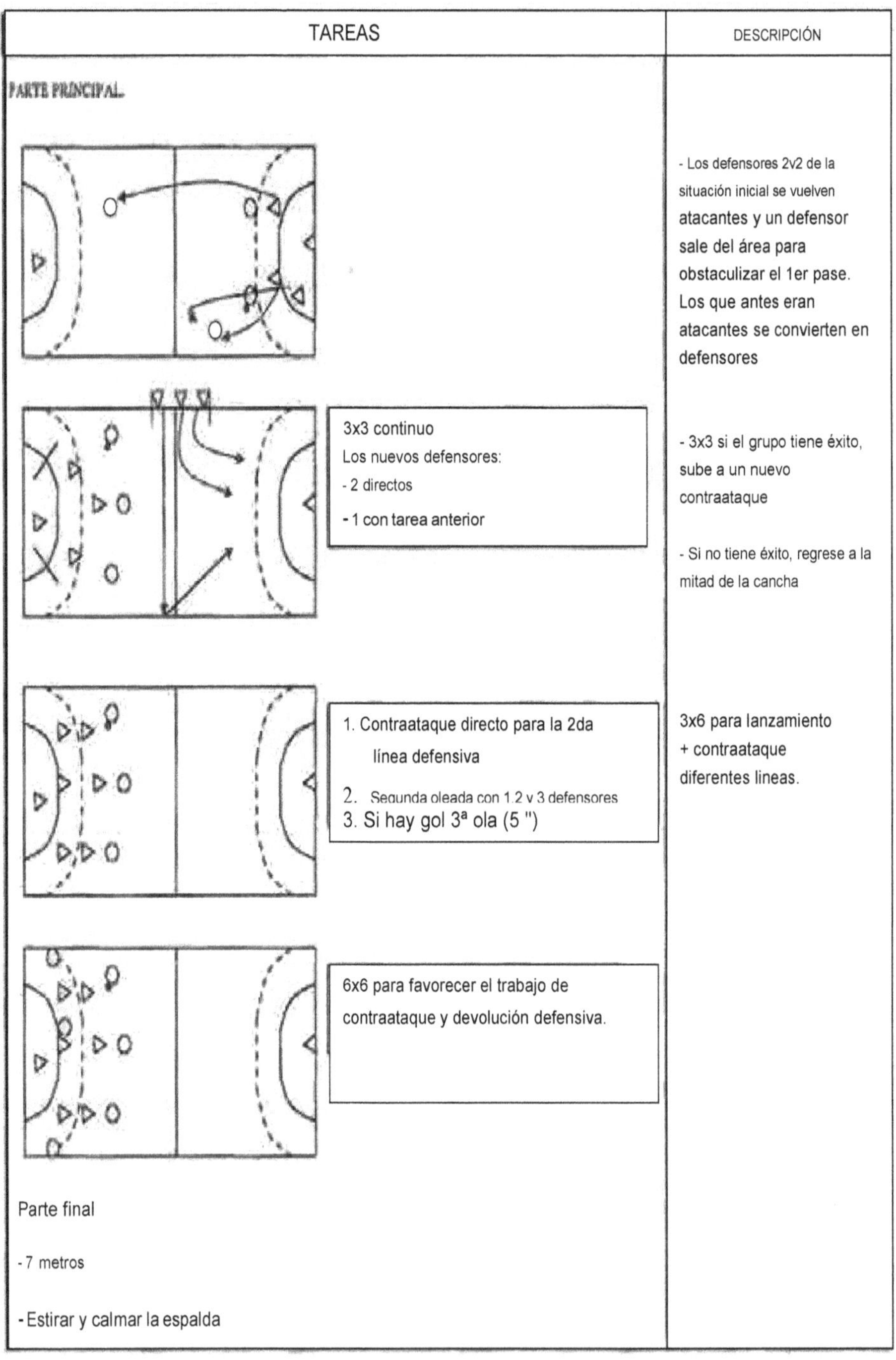

PARTE PRINCIPAL

3x3 continuo
Los nuevos defensores:
- 2 directos
- 1 con tarea anterior

- Los defensores 2v2 de la situación inicial se vuelven atacantes y un defensor sale del área para obstaculizar el 1er pase. Los que antes eran atacantes se convierten en defensores

- 3x3 si el grupo tiene éxito, sube a un nuevo contraataque

- Si no tiene éxito, regrese a la mitad de la cancha

1. Contraataque directo para la 2da línea defensiva
2. Segunda oleada con 1.2 v 3 defensores
3. Si hay gol 3ª ola (5 ")

3x6 para lanzamiento + contraataque diferentes lineas.

6x6 para favorecer el trabajo de contraataque y devolución defensiva.

Parte final

- 7 metros

- Estirar y calmar la espalda

OBJETIVO GENERAL

Tec-Tac del SISTEMA DEFENSIVO 3:3

PROPÓSITO ESPECÍFICO

- Filosofía, principios básicos, espacios especiales   cíclicos.

TAREAS	DESCRIPCIÓN

Calefacción
- Libre por parejas defendiendo ambos desplazamientos,   estirando

- Grupo de 4
      2x2 marcando diferentes goles 2 balones

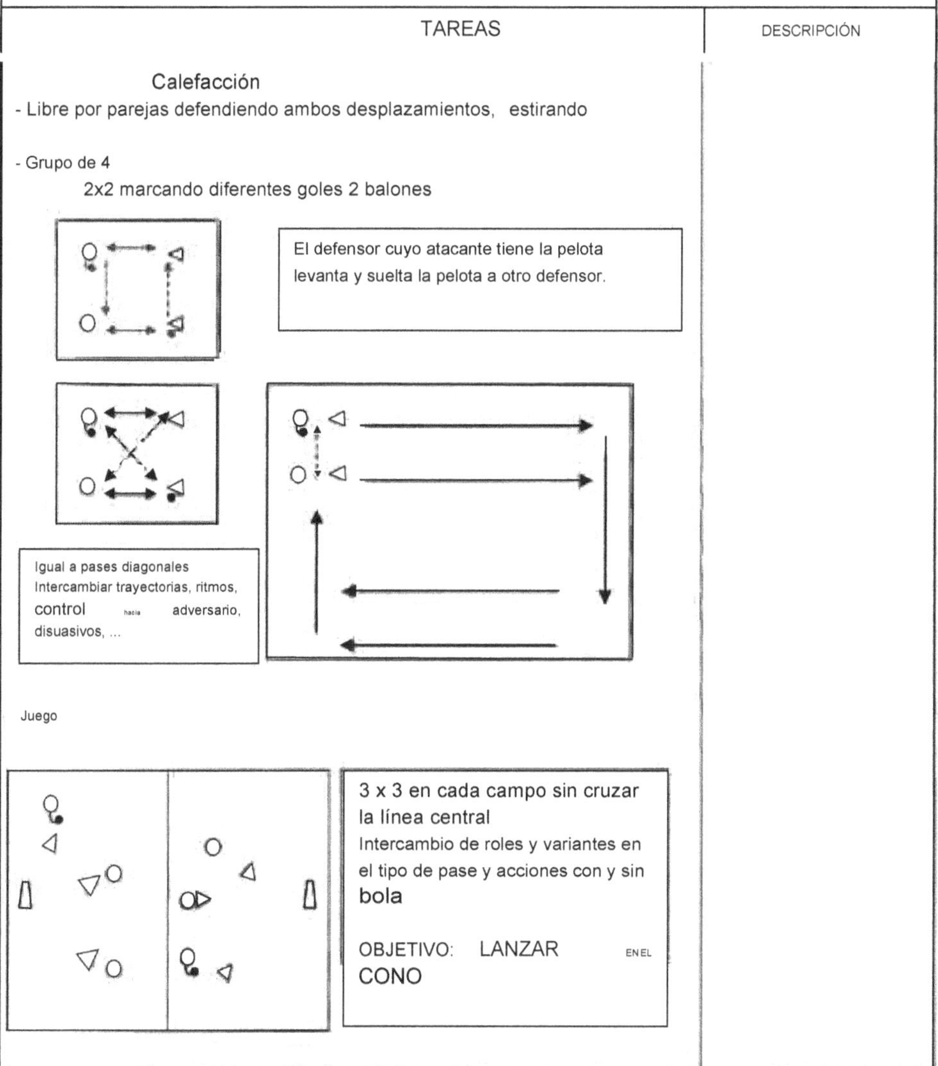

El defensor cuyo atacante tiene la pelota
levanta y suelta la pelota a otro defensor.

Igual a pases diagonales
Intercambiar trayectorias, ritmos,
control   hacia   adversario,
disuasivos, ...

Juego

3 x 3 en cada campo sin cruzar
la línea central
Intercambio de roles y variantes en
el tipo de pase y acciones con y sin
bola

OBJETIVO: LANZAR   EN EL
CONO

TAREAS	DESCRIPCIÓN

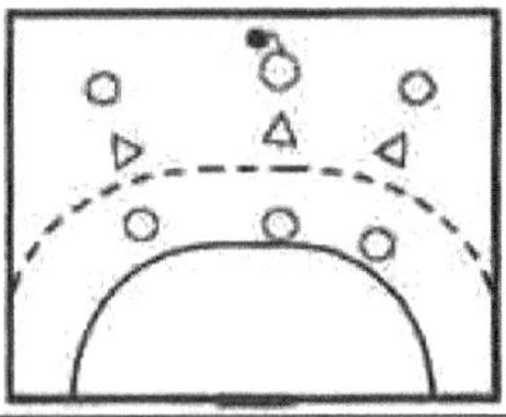

Juego 3x3 + posibilidad de pase al pívot del mismo lado. Defensores: desplazamientos, líneas de paso, anticipaciones

Portero calentando

parte principal

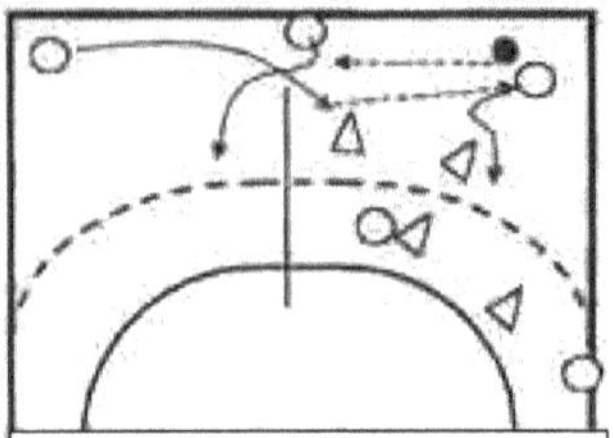

Obra 4x4 desde cruces, intercambios ... con lateral en el lado opuesto.

Enfoque: respuesta a la circulación extrema.

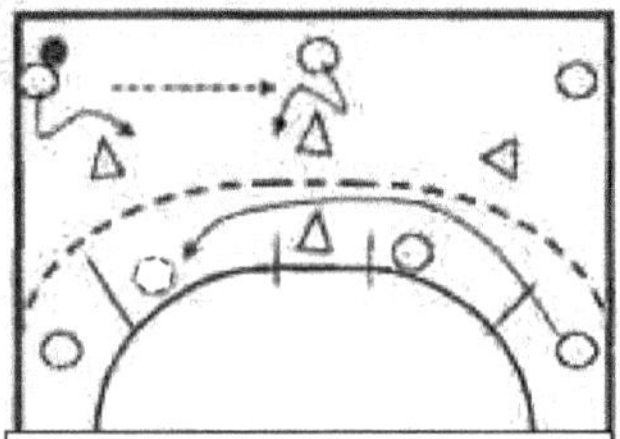

Defensa 4x4
Posibilidad de movimiento de los extremos y juego 5x4
Líneas de pase / Estructura defensiva

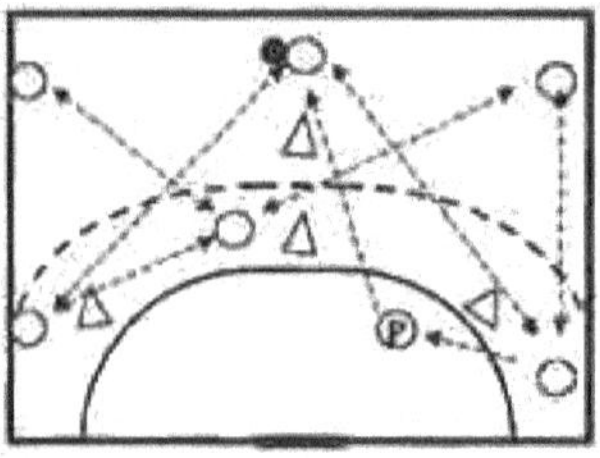

Juego 4x4:
Cuando un jugador pasa al portero de apoyo, los defensores orientan el balón
El portero busca pasar a otros compañeros y trabajo con lanzamiento.
Importante: Pautas, desplazamientos, adecuación de defensores.

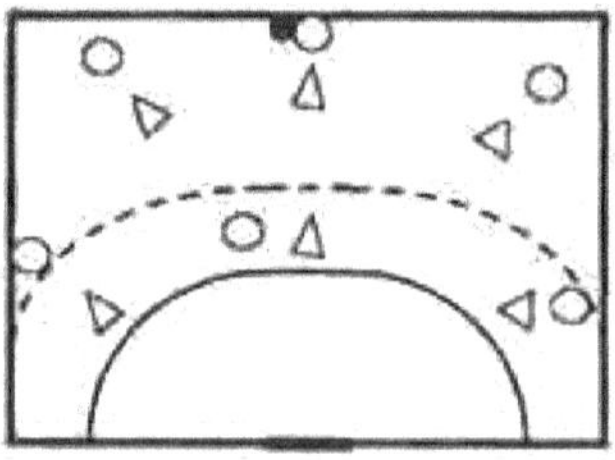

Vuelve con calma.

Juego 6x6

A. No se despliega ningún pivote
B. Circulación de extremos,
   entrada de 1ª fila en pivote.

OBJETIVO GENERAL

Introducción a los sistemas defensivos

3: 2: 1 y 5: 1

PROPÓSITO ESPECÍFICO

- Filosofía, principios básicos, espacios   específicos.

TAREAS	DESCRIPCIÓN

Calefacción
   - gratis con pelota
Tareas:
- regate
- emisiones de aire + recepciones
- manipulación con manos y pies

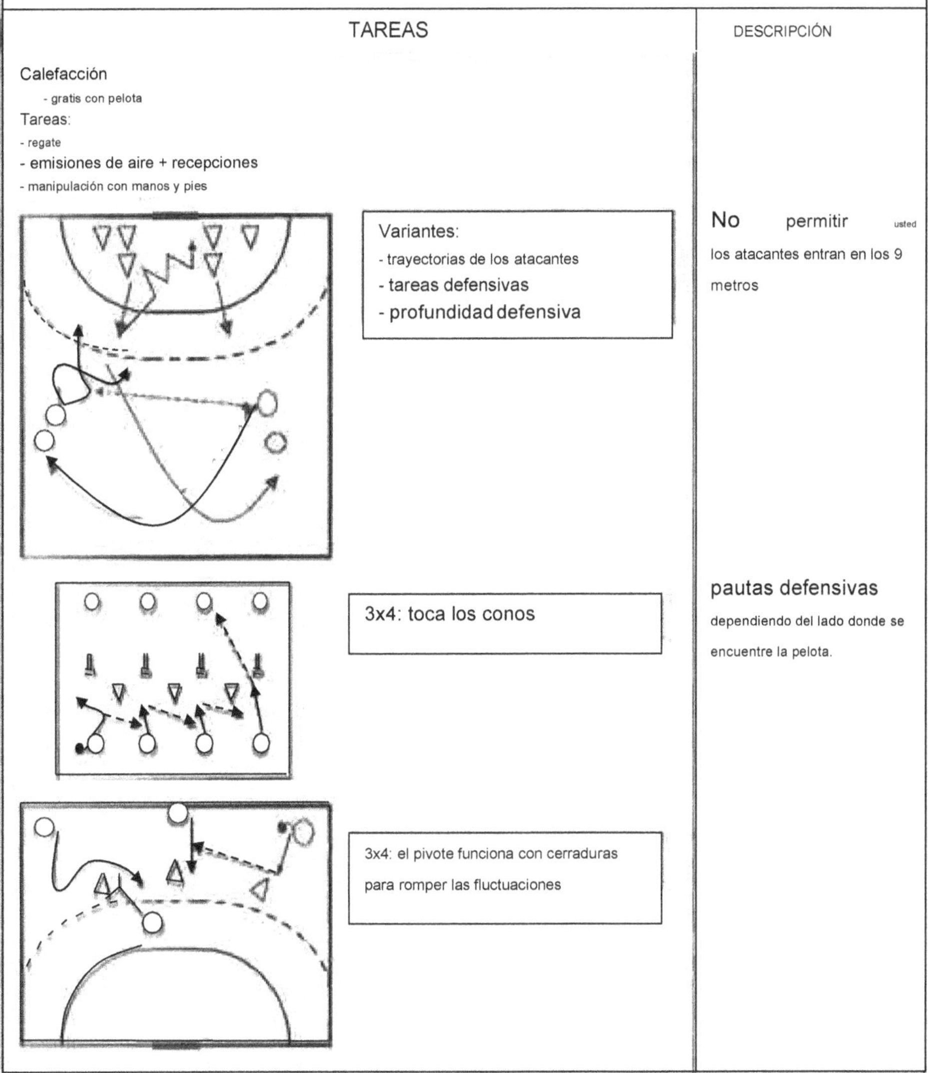

Variantes:
- trayectorias de los atacantes
- tareas defensivas
- profundidad defensiva

No permitir usted los atacantes entran en los 9 metros

3x4: toca los conos

pautas defensivas

dependiendo del lado donde se encuentre la pelota.

3x4: el pivote funciona con cerraduras para romper las fluctuaciones

TAREAS	DESCRIPCIÓN

Portero calentando

parte principal

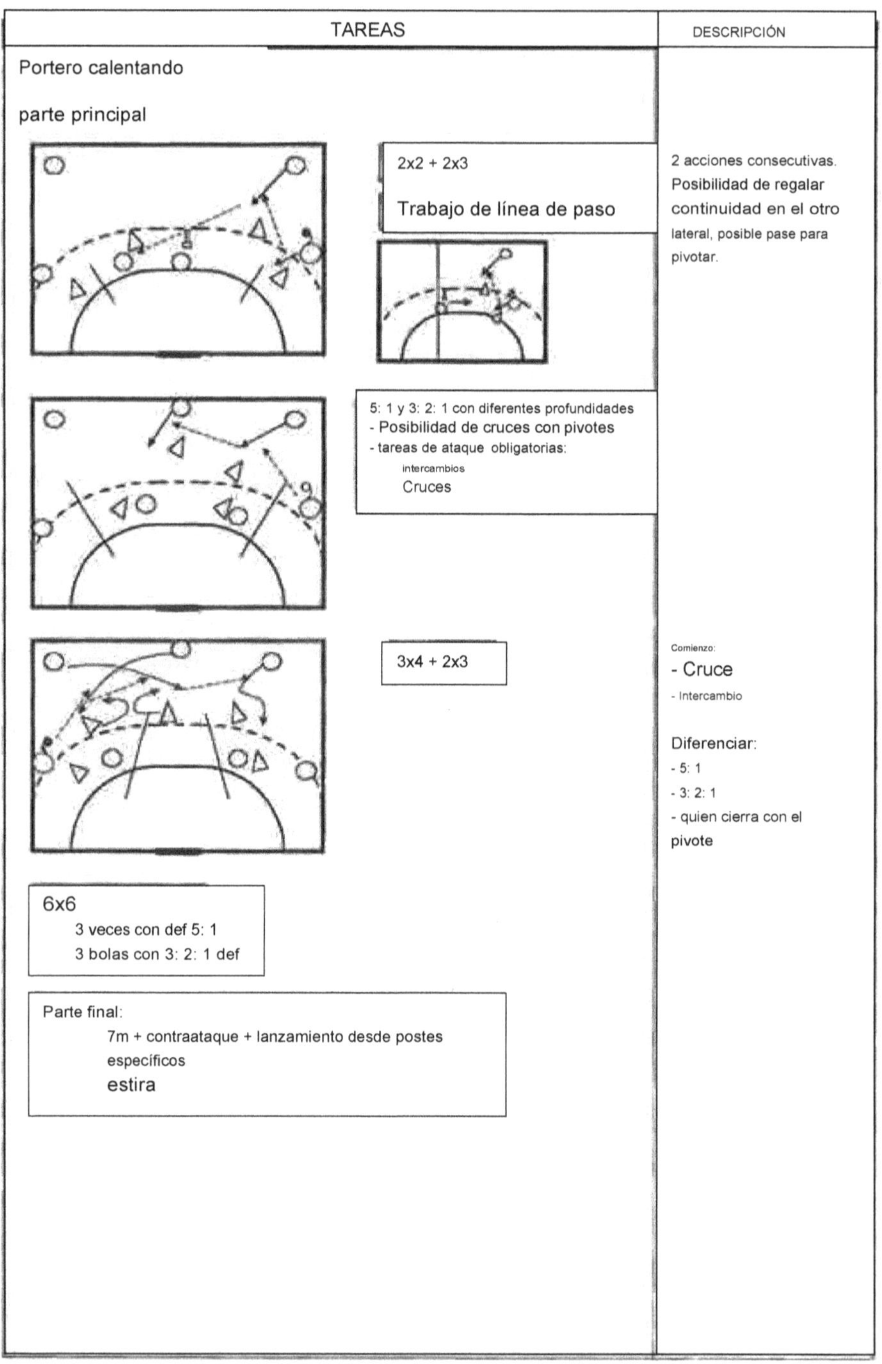

2 acciones consecutivas. Posibilidad de regalar continuidad en el otro lateral, posible pase para pivotar.

Comienzo:
- Cruce
- Intercambio

Diferenciar:
- 5: 1
- 3: 2: 1
- quien cierra con el pivote

6x6
    3 veces con def 5: 1
    3 bolas con 3: 2: 1 def

Parte final:
    7m + contraataque + lanzamiento desde postes
    específicos
    estira

OBJETIVO GENERAL

Procedimientos de ataque táctico colectivo
Sistemas defensivos 6: 0 y 5: 1
PROPÓSITO ESPECÍFICO

- Cerraduras, Contra-cerraduras y coordinación
- Procedimientos tácticos colectivos ofensivos

TAREAS	DESCRIPCIÓN

Calefacción:
- Gratis (cada jugador con una pelota individualmente)
- Juego (fútbol de mano)
    - Fuera del área: reglas de balonmano
    - Dentro del área: solo juega con tus pies

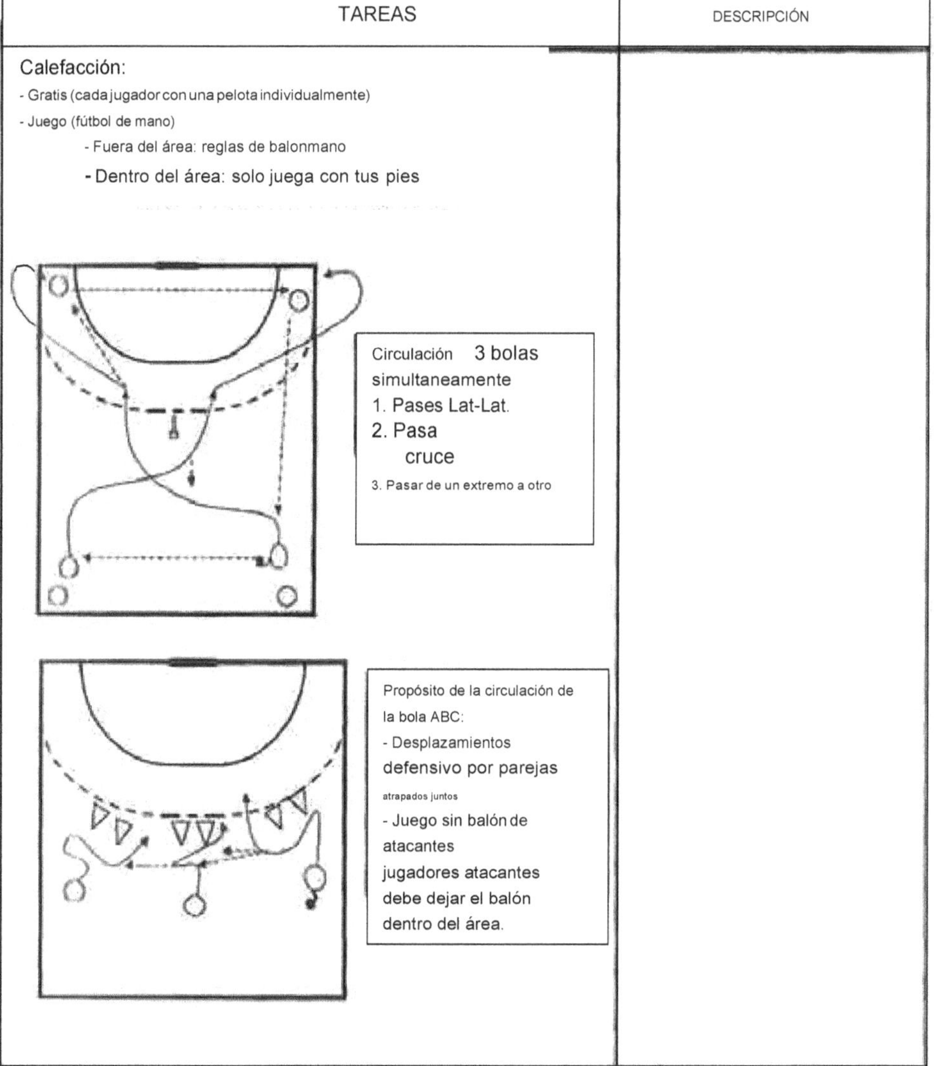

TAREAS	DESCRIPCIÓN

Calentamiento del portero

Juego 2v2 (de pie con 2 defensores)
Juego 2v2 (pivote central con bloqueo de 2 defensores)
Posibilidad de pase de pivote lateral y juego 2x2

Juego 2x2 (delantero-trasero) (cruces y fijaciones) y los atacantes van al bando contrario para defender 3x2 BCD con penetraciones sucesivas. Entre las dos acciones, el portero cambia a B para iniciar el 3x2

Juego 4x4: Iniciación de puntos con penetraciones sucesivas aprovechando los bloqueos de pivote. El primer defensor comienza con un pequeño desequilibrio inicial cuando Intenta defender la banda con el balón.

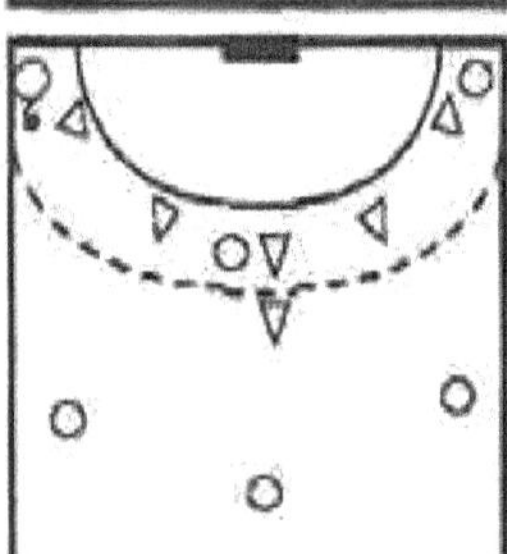

Juego 6x6:
- Defensa 6: 0 (con suficiente profundidad)
- Defensa 5: 1

Con o sin fracturas
Marcar goles ofensivos y defensivos generales

TACTICA INDIVIDUAL (1:1)

	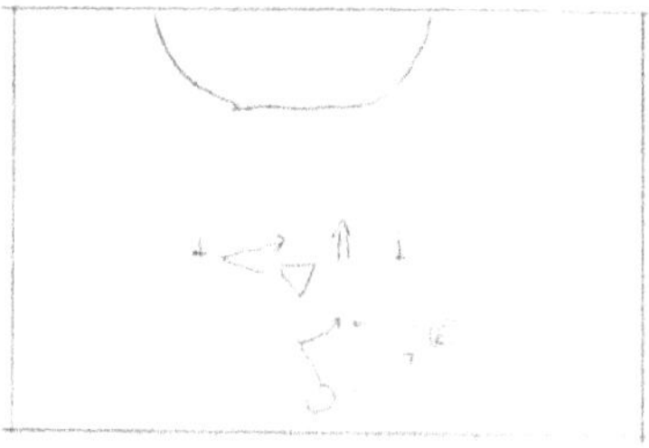	Buena técnica. Ataque Defensa No luchar contra las reglas Responsabilidad total espacio y oponente
	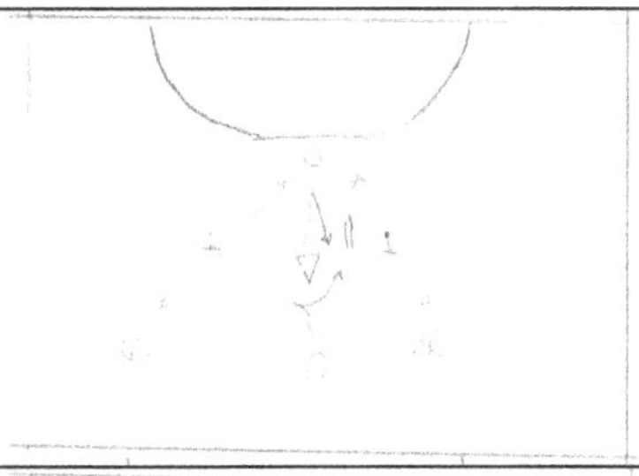	Variedad de acciones Problemas diferentes Pivote Primera línea
	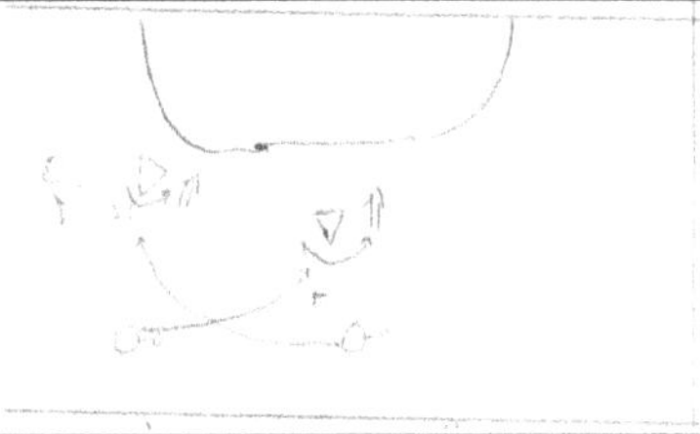	Mas jugadores involucrados. Trayectorias y distancias correctas.
	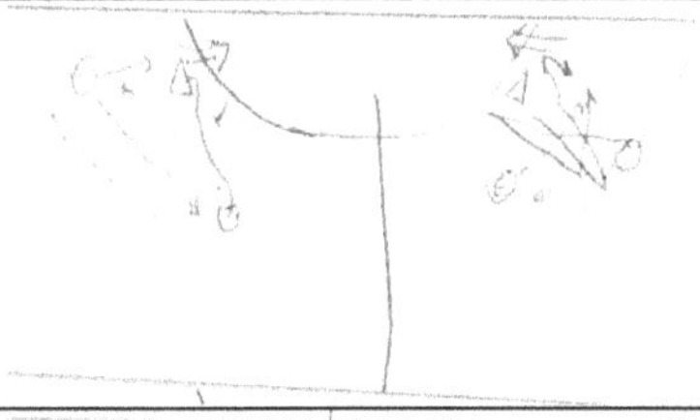	Use el primer ejercicio en la posición de extremo.

		1:1 defensor trata de tocar el jugador con balón. Si lo toca cuando remata y es gol el atacante gana.

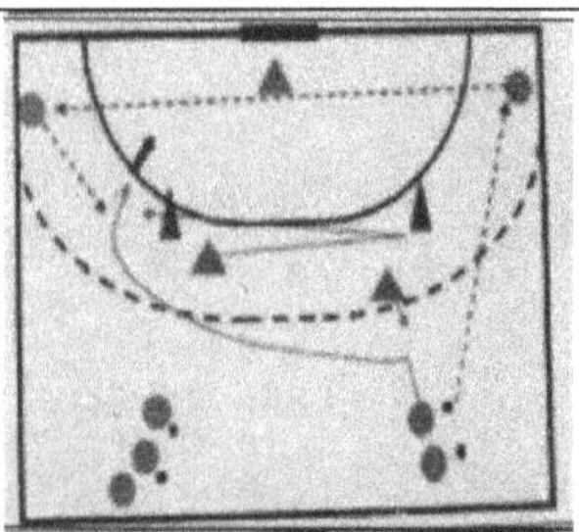 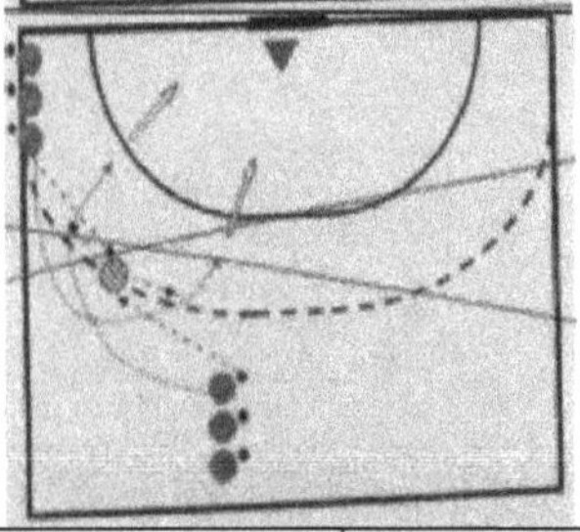	Orientarse para fintar o lanzar
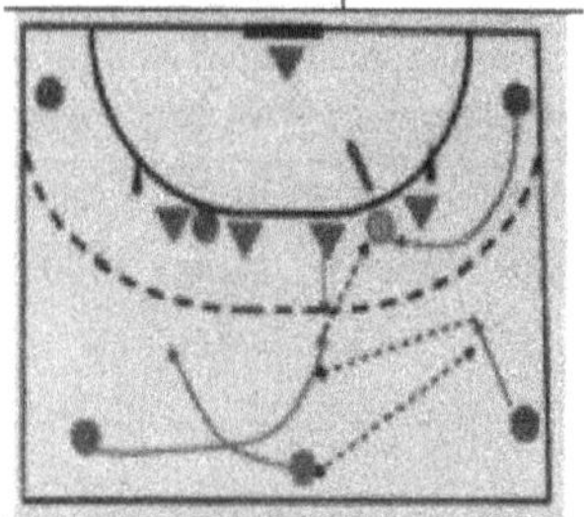	4:4 + 1 jugador 5:4 Gol en 4 pases.
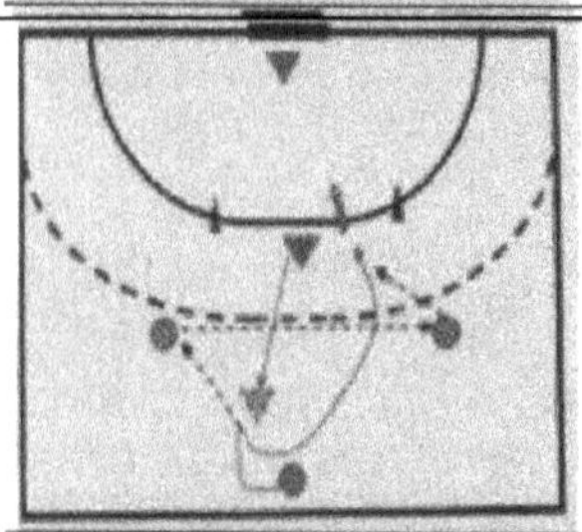	1:1 con 2 pases. El defensor trata de tocar al atacante con el balón. Si es tocado cuando tira y es gol, el atacante gano.
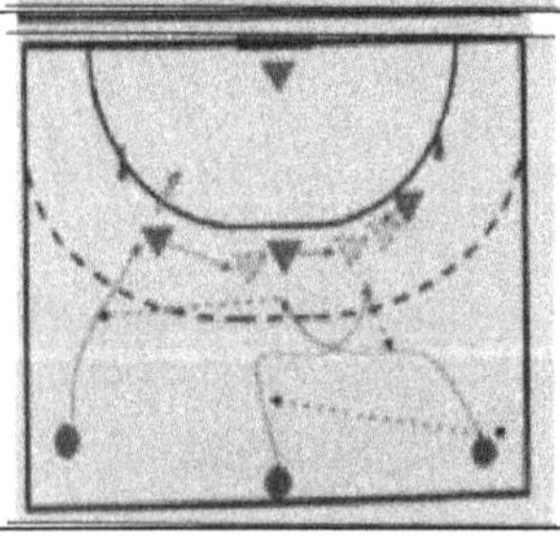	Uso de fijación. Fijación par – cruce Fijación impar Desmarque.

PROCEDIMIENTOS TACTICOS (2:2)

Trabajo y continuidad hasta que haya una clara oportunidad.
Pivote
　　　Bloqueo estático 6m
　　　Bloqueo dinámico 9m
Primera línea
　　　Posición de remate
　　　Atacar portería

Progresiones sucesivas
Cruces

3:3
2:2 + 1:1

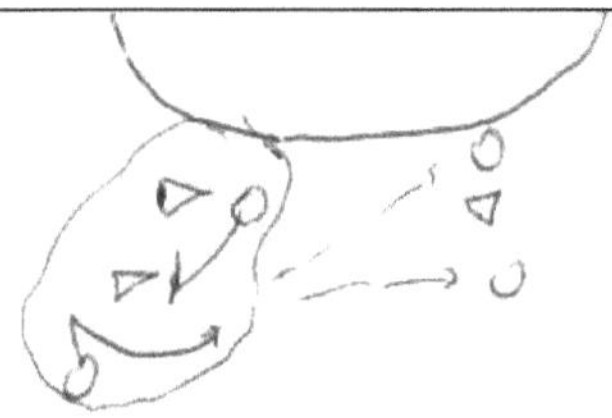	2:2 + continuidad
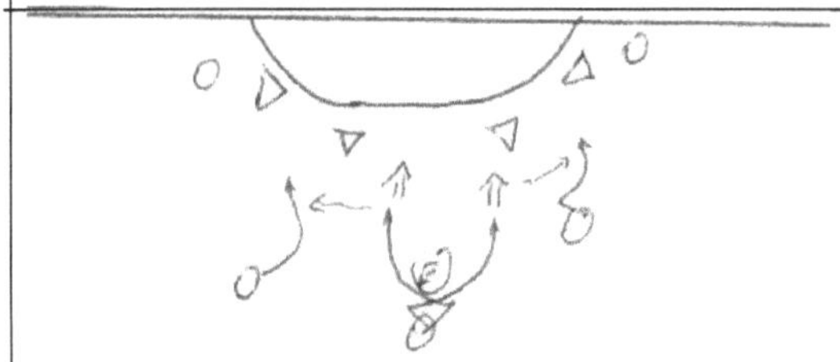	5:4
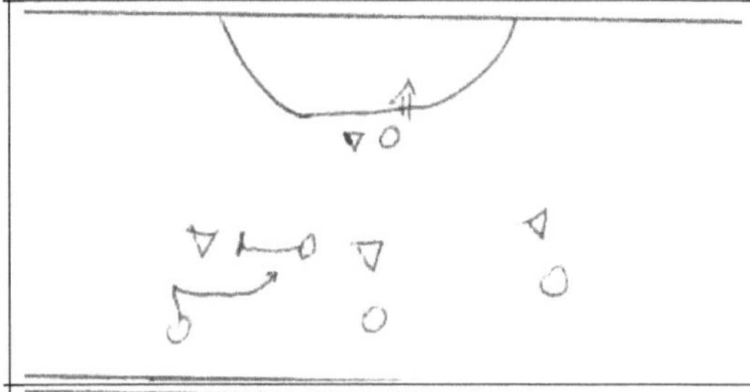	3:3 + 1:1 Pivote en 2 líneas
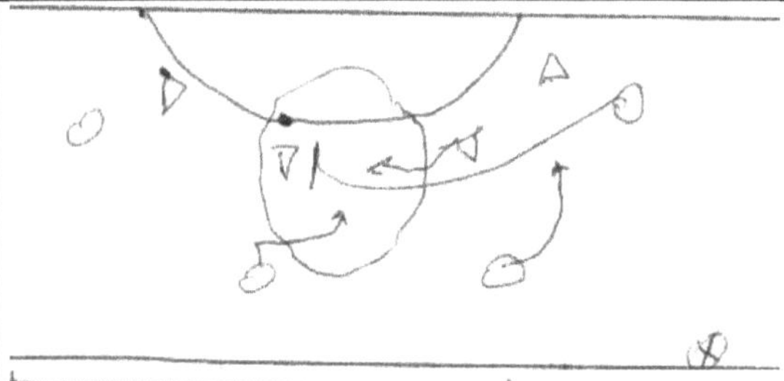 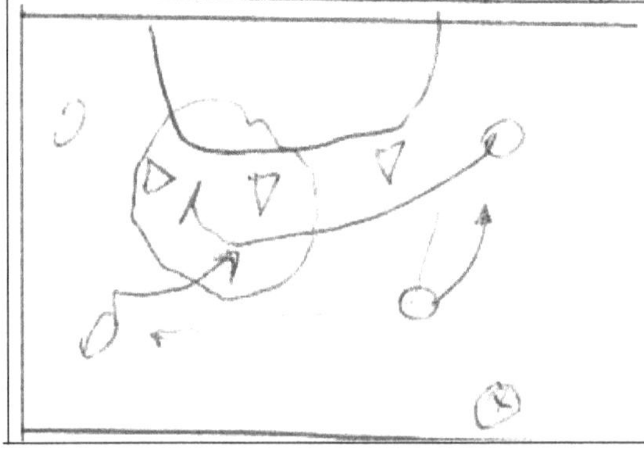	4:4 Cualquiera puede entrar a 2-4 2:2 + continuidad

		3:3 Pase y va Cruces sin balón utilizando el espacio creado antes.
		6:4 El central juega solo con el pivote.

MEJORA FIJACIONES

		No atacar al oponente. Atacar los espacios entre ellos. Acciones cortas con balón. Ambigüedad pasando el balón.

		3:2 previo movimiento de los atacantes.
		2 pases después de recibir del entrenador.
		Orientación de los pies hacia la portería.
		Gestos no superfluos.
		Brazo armado.
		Progresión:
		      Reducir los pases
		      Reducir los pasos

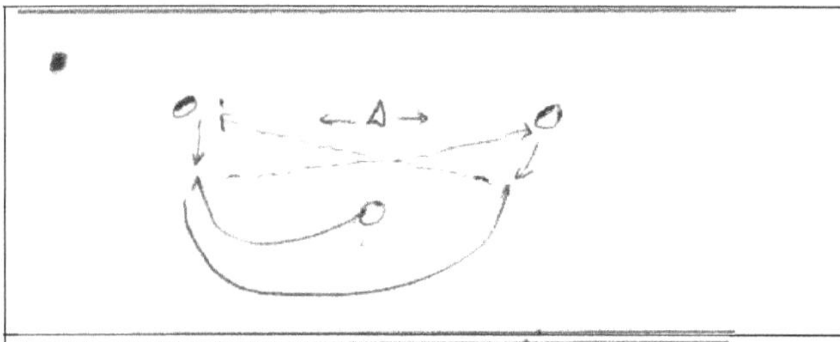	Pases tensos Trayectorias largas. Timing con el balón.
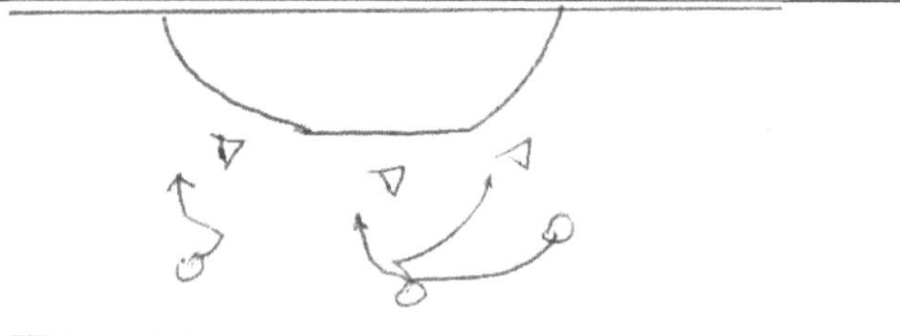	Fijación par – Cruce Fijación impar – Desmarque indirecto.
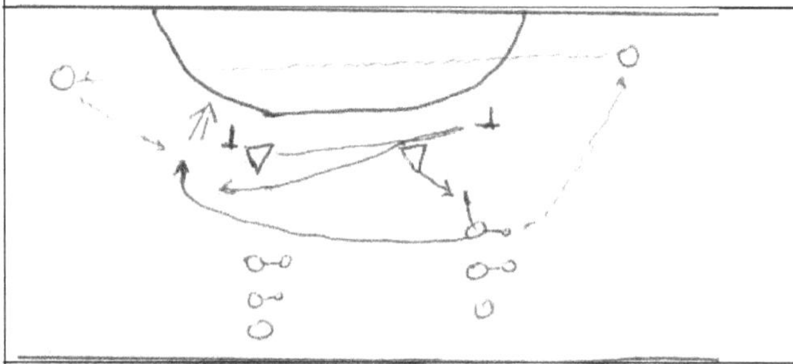	Orientación para lanzar. Duelo con el oponente.
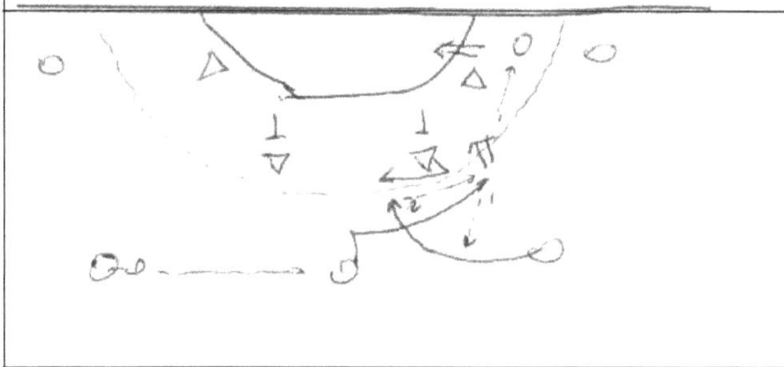	5:4 Superioridad después del cruce en la zona central. Lanzamientos solo desde 9 m.
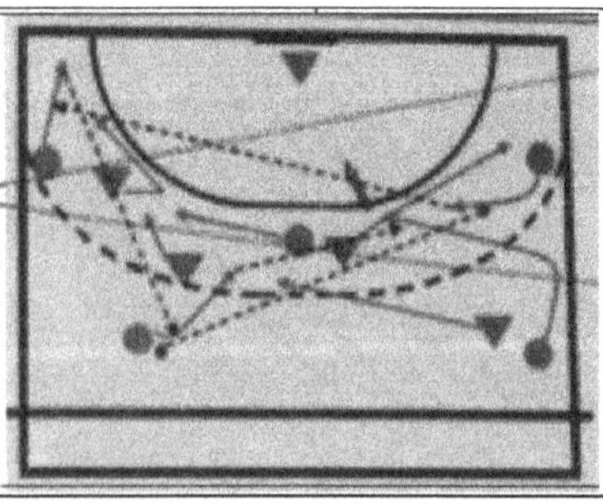	6:5 o 5:4 Sin ser tocado Progresión, un bote o solo un paso. Campo visual. Pasar y recibir en movimiento y atacar la portería.

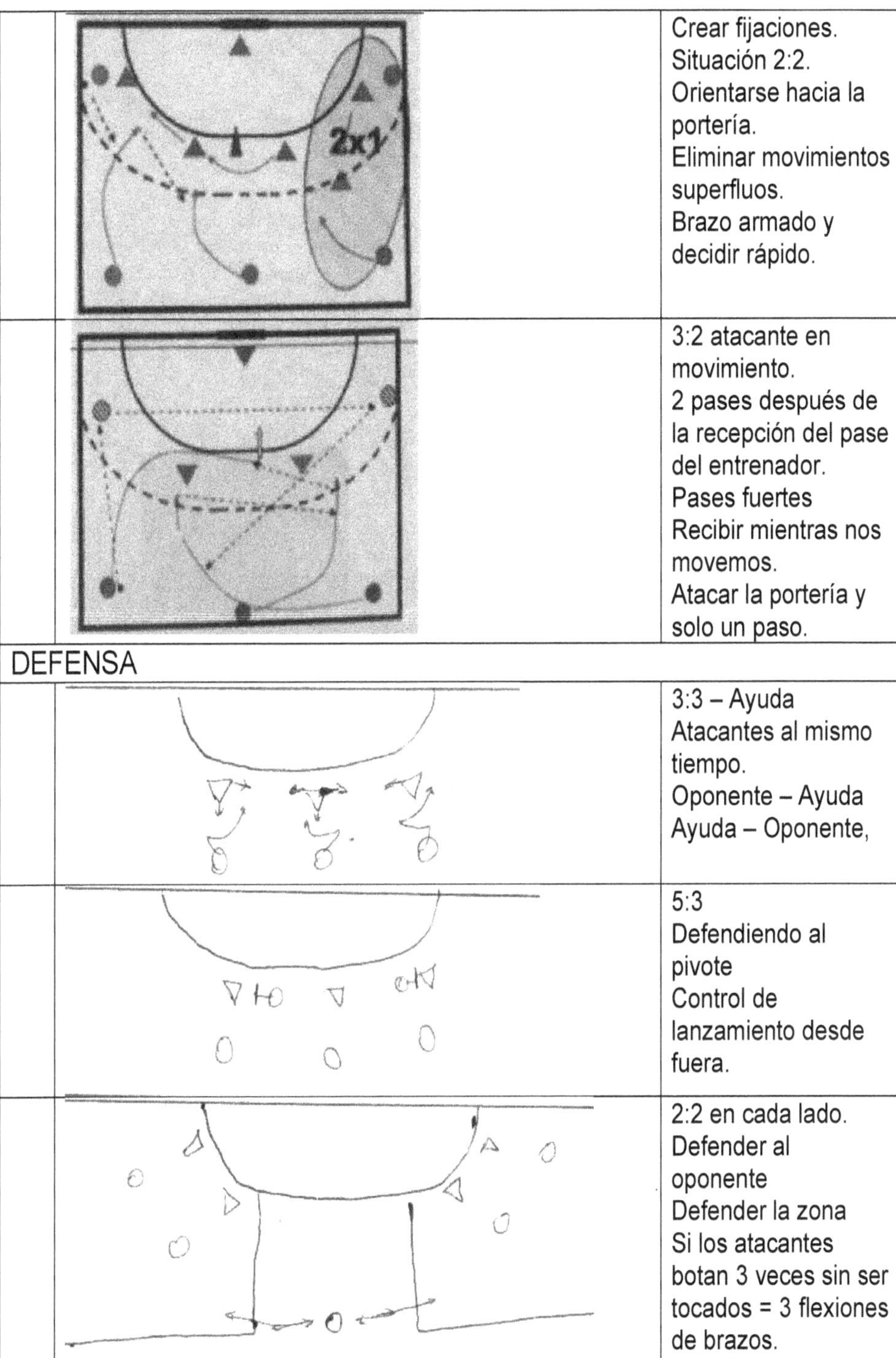

	Crear fijaciones. Situación 2:2. Orientarse hacia la portería. Eliminar movimientos superfluos. Brazo armado y decidir rápido.
	3:2 atacante en movimiento. 2 pases después de la recepción del pase del entrenador. Pases fuertes Recibir mientras nos movemos. Atacar la portería y solo un paso.

DEFENSA

	3:3 – Ayuda Atacantes al mismo tiempo. Oponente – Ayuda Ayuda – Oponente,
	5:3 Defendiendo al pivote Control de lanzamiento desde fuera.
	2:2 en cada lado. Defender al oponente Defender la zona Si los atacantes botan 3 veces sin ser tocados = 3 flexiones de brazos.

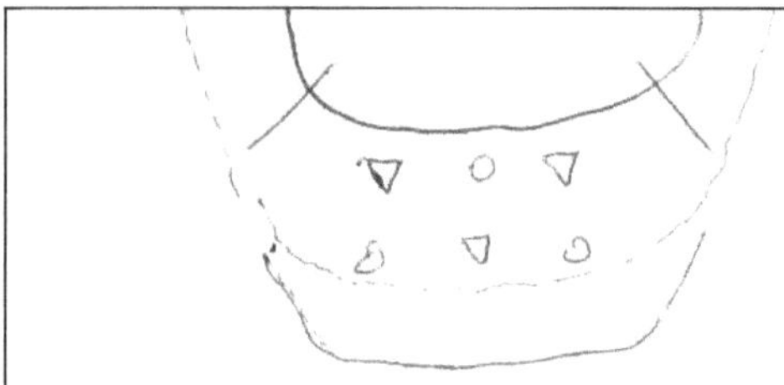	3:3 Atacantes pueden moverse hacia atrás máximo hasta la zona extra. Si botan 3 veces tienen que ser tocado.
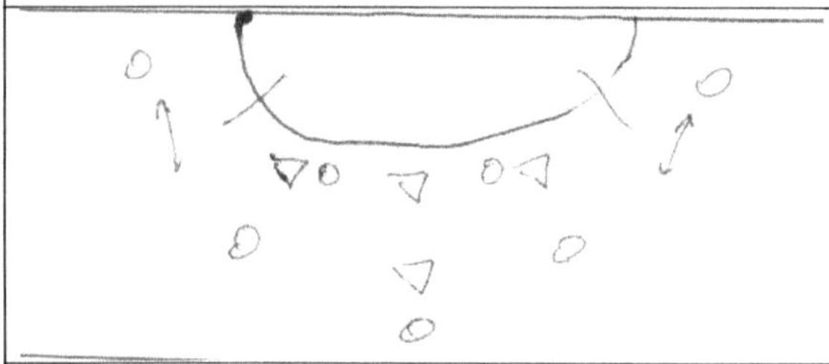	5:4 Si no hay gol en 4 pases, pase al extremo y empezar de nuevo.
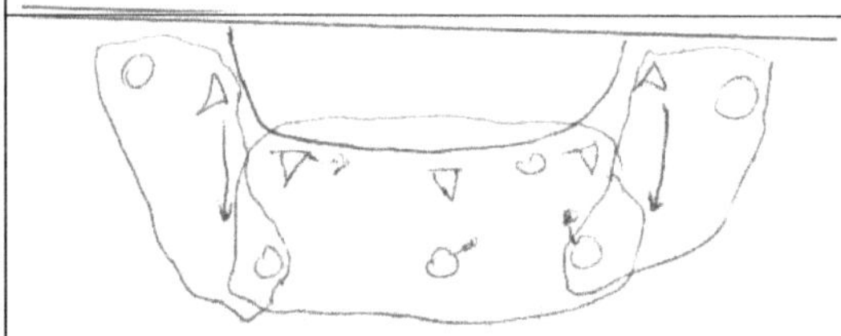	3:4 en el centro 1:2 en el extremo cuando el balón esta en el lado opuesto.
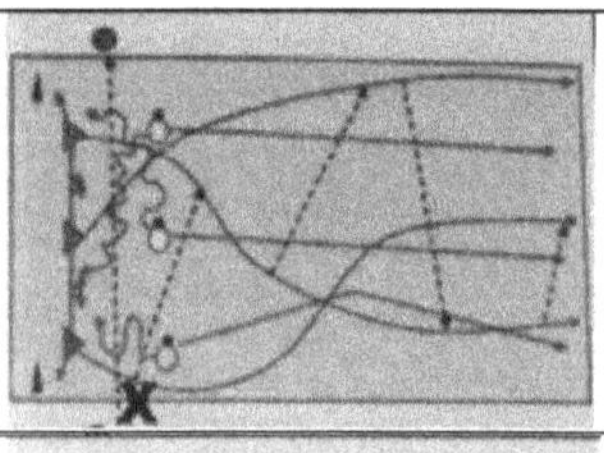	3:3 Defender una puerta Interceptar y contra ataque
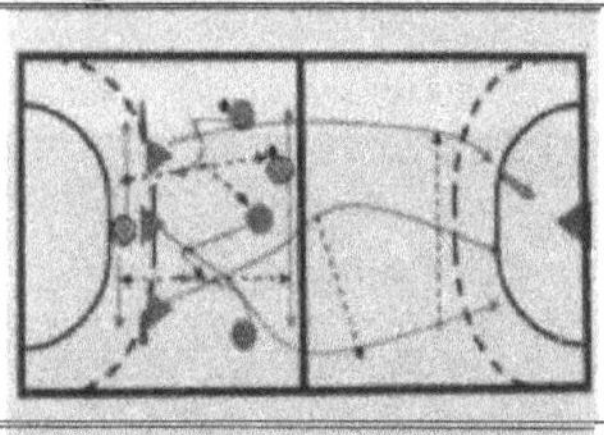	Defender e interceptar el pase al pivote y contra ataque 2:2
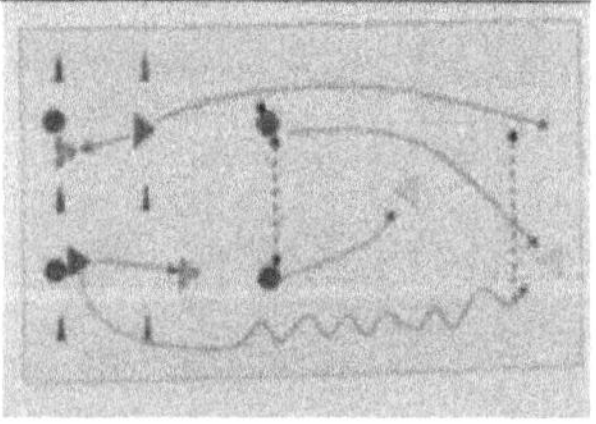	Defensa de una puerta y el pivot El atacante puede pasar el balón al pivote en el lado opuesto. Si interceptamos contra ataque.

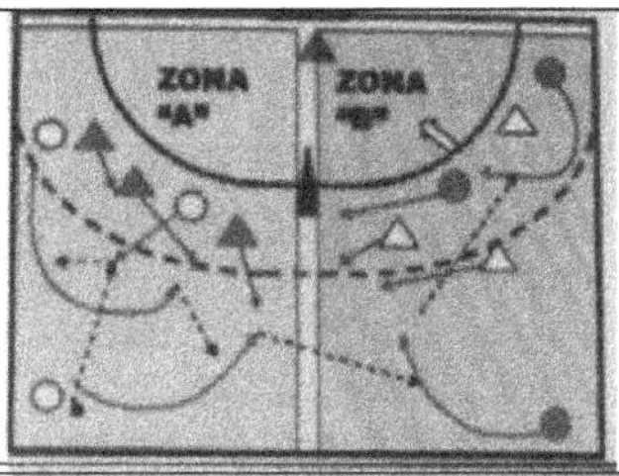 ZONA "A" ZONA "B"		2 zonas – 3:3 en cada una Los atacantes pueden pasar un máximo de 5 veces y sino pasar al otro lado.
		Defensores que reciben el gol primero pierden. Bloqueos 4:4 con 2 apoyos en los extremos Goles penetrando o desde el pivot = 1 punto Goles desde fuera 3 puntos
		Intercepciones estáticas
		4:3 Intercepciones y Ayudas
		Defender el castillo. Los atacantes tratan de entrar en el cuadrado con el balón y los defensores tratan de evitarlo. 2 atacantes no pueden atacar la misma puerta,

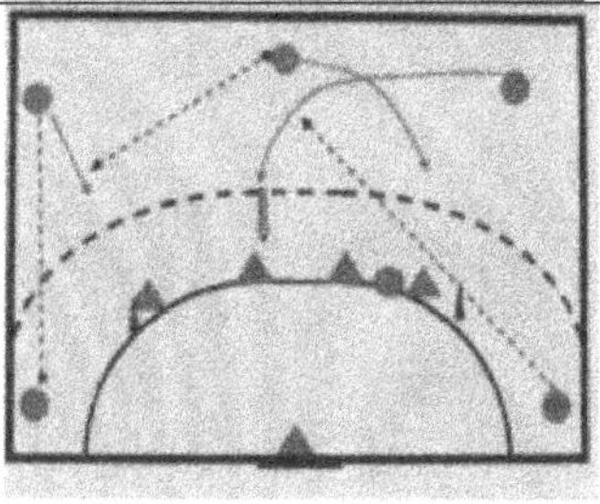

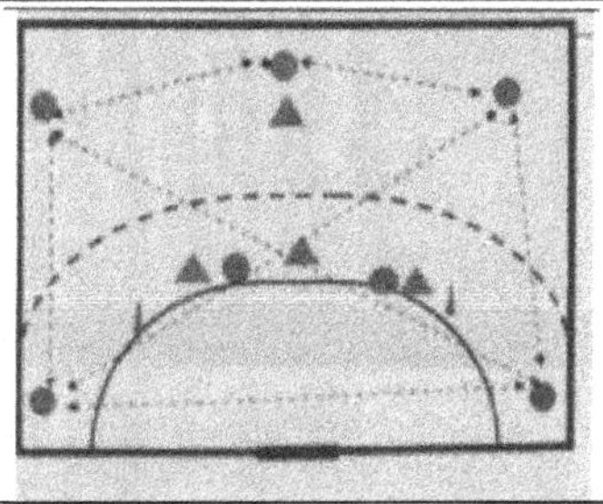

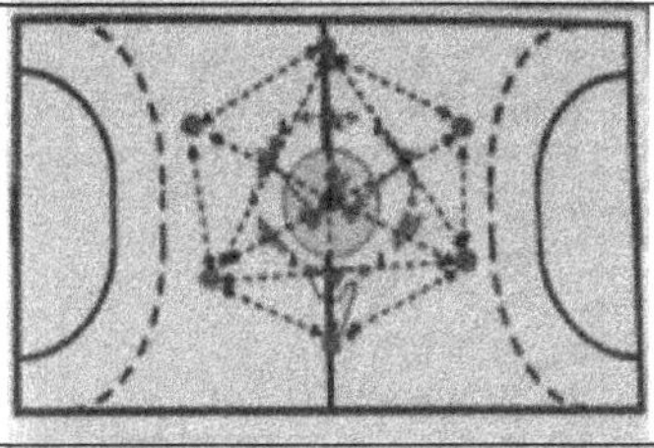

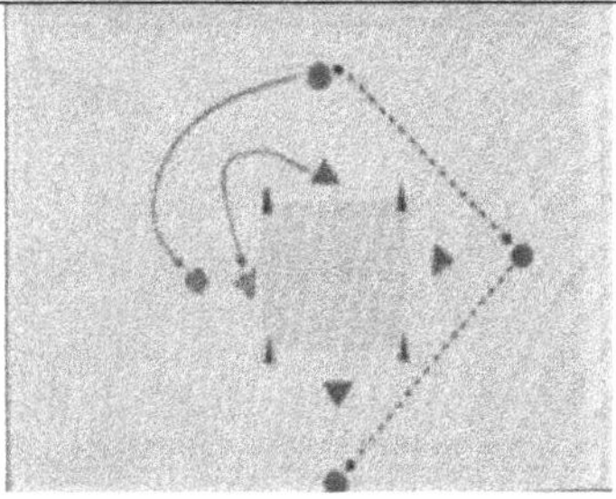

		Cuantos pases podemos defender 4:5 antes del gol.
		1:1 + marcaje a pivote Defender la puerta cuando el oponente tiene el balón Cuan el balón esta en el otro lado marcar al pivote.
		1:1 defender la puerta e interceptar. Defender normalmente Marcar el desplazamiento del oponente y algunas veces intentar interceptar los pases
		Marcar e interceptar Interceptar el pase entre 2 atacantes sin dejar de marcar el pivote. Cuando el pase va al atacante de fuera debemos defender la puerta.
		Defensa 1:2 y retorno defensivo.

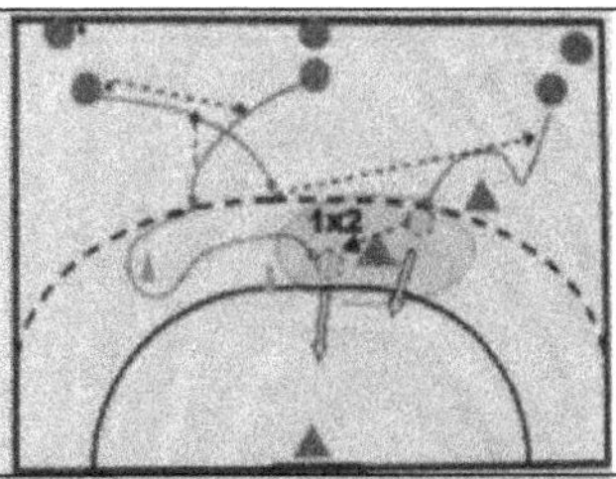	Defensa 1:2
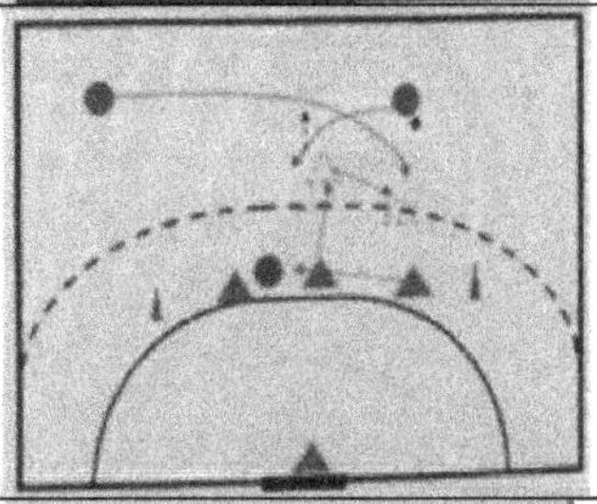	Defensa 1:2 y cruce.
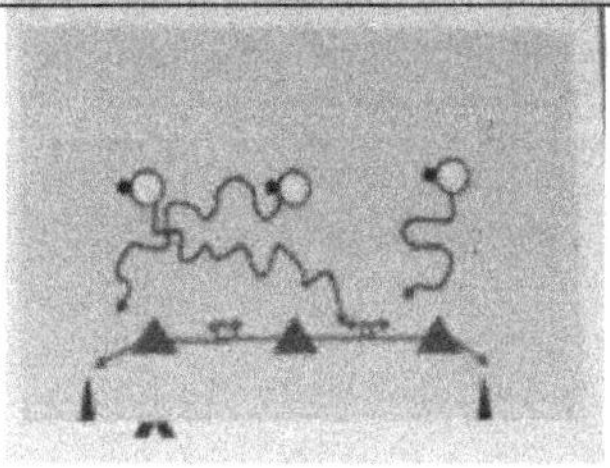	Defensa de la puerta 3:3 Atacantes botando continuamente. Defensa debe prevenir a los atacantes entrar en la puerta. Todos los defensores están 1:1 pero tienen que ayudar 3:3
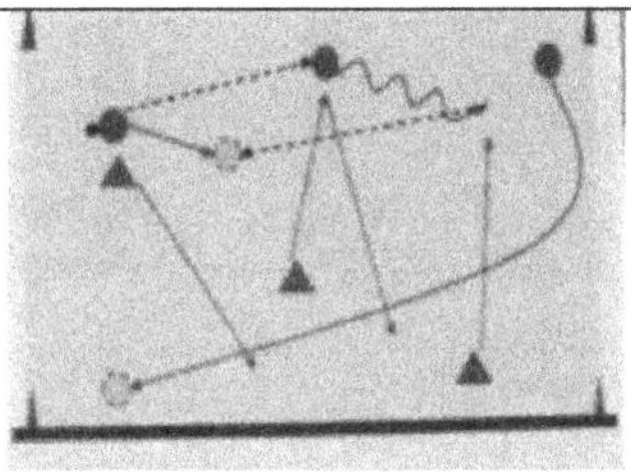	Defender la puerta y una zona profunda. Defensores deben evitar a los atacantes pasar la puerta. Si el atacante dribla 3 veces sin ser tocado gana.
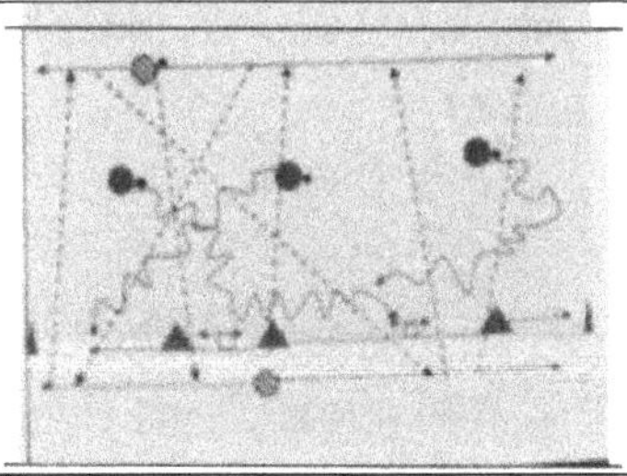	Defensa de una puerta 3:3 Interceptar los pases.

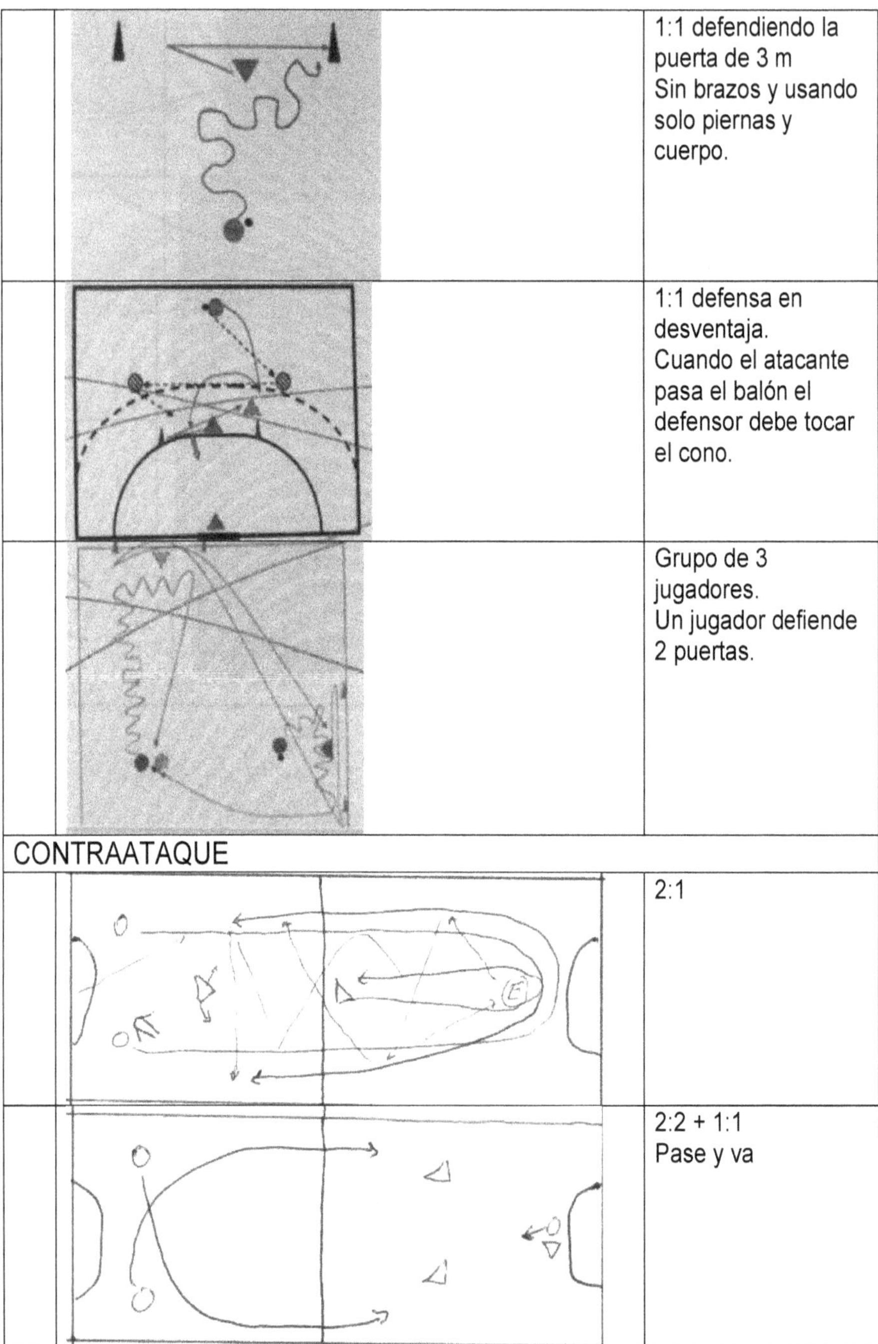

	1:1 defendiendo la puerta de 3 m Sin brazos y usando solo piernas y cuerpo.
	1:1 defensa en desventaja. Cuando el atacante pasa el balón el defensor debe tocar el cono.
	Grupo de 3 jugadores. Un jugador defiende 2 puertas.

CONTRAATAQUE

| | 2:1 |
| | 2:2 + 1:1
Pase y va |

3:2 + 3:2

3:3
6 pases
Pase de portero
contraataque
3:3 medio campo
3:2

3:3
Corre detrás de los
defensores sin balón
(Ganar la espalda)

3:3
Pressing medio
campo
3:3 + 3:3
Jugadores jugando
solos medio campo

1:1
3 balones

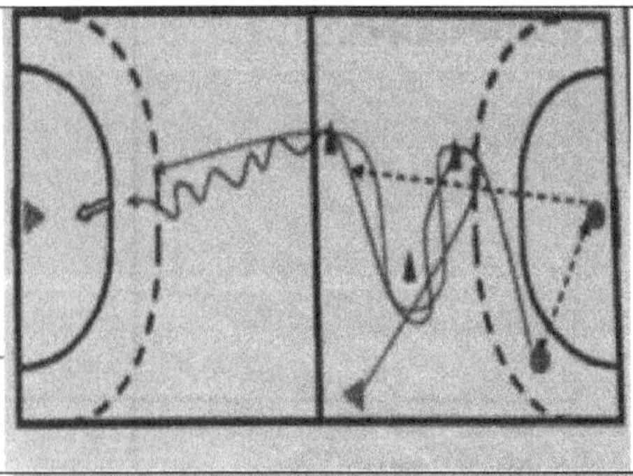	1:0 Finalización del contraataque
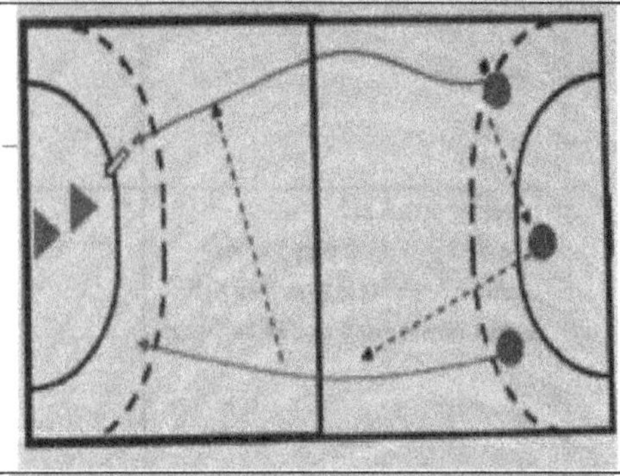	1:2 Finalizacion
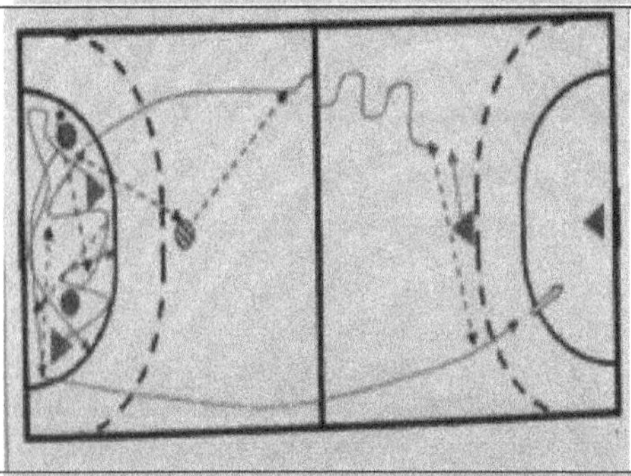	Contraataque 2:1 3 pases con oposición dentro de el área. Pase al compañero y contraataque
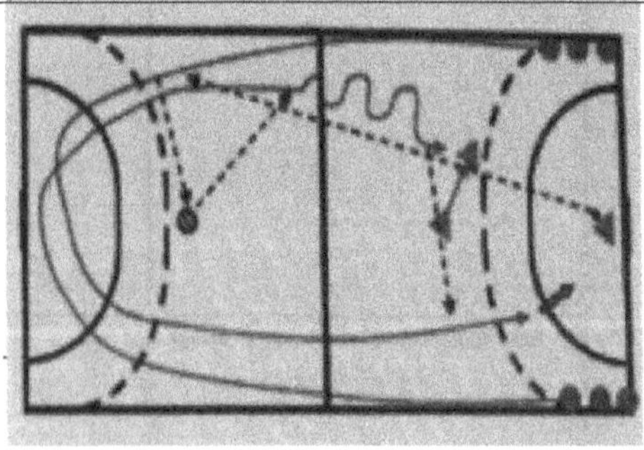	2:1 Espacios grandes

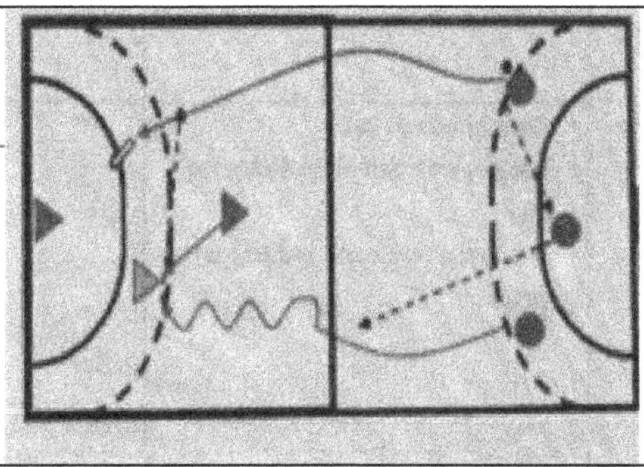	Contraataque 2:1 Defensa en nuestra mitad del campo. El pasador debe hacerlo de forma que el atacante reciba el balón antes de pasar medio campo.
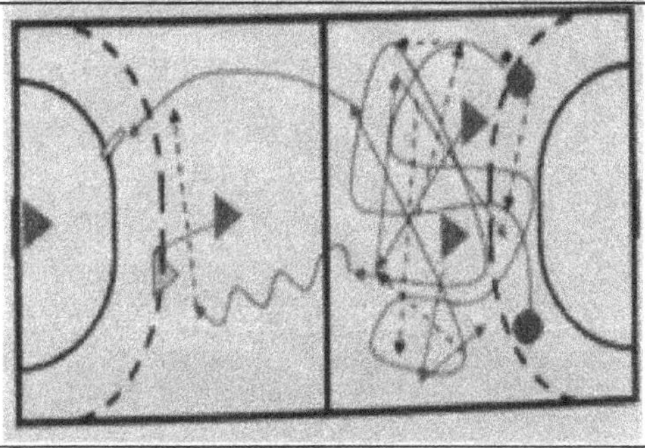	Contraataque 2:1 Los atacantes deben de pasar 5 veces. Sin driblar en su propio campo antes de pasar al campo del adversario.
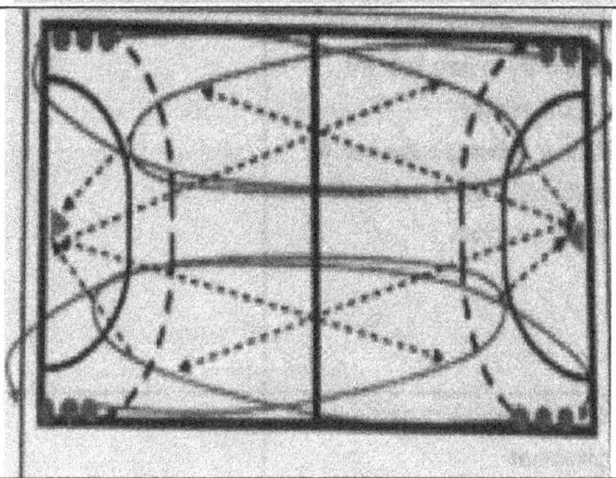	Contraataque con pases largos y retorno defensivo.
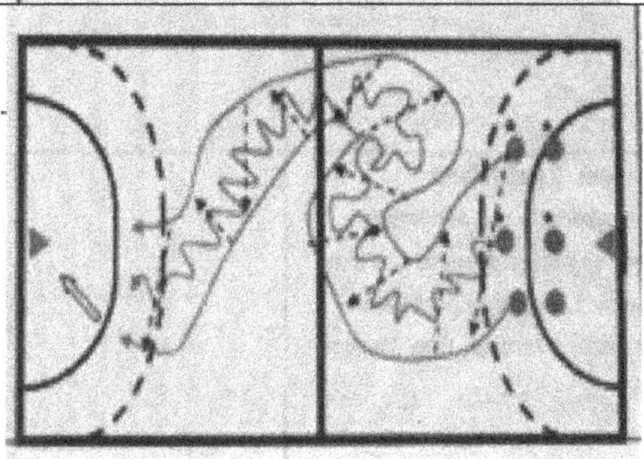	Grupos de 3 jugadores con 2 balones Un jugador bota a máxima velocidad con cambios continuos de dirección. Los otros 2 le siguen pasandose.

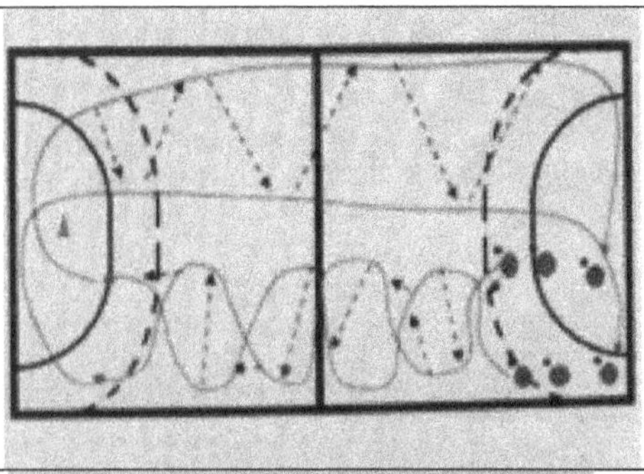	Ida sin cruces Retorno con cruces
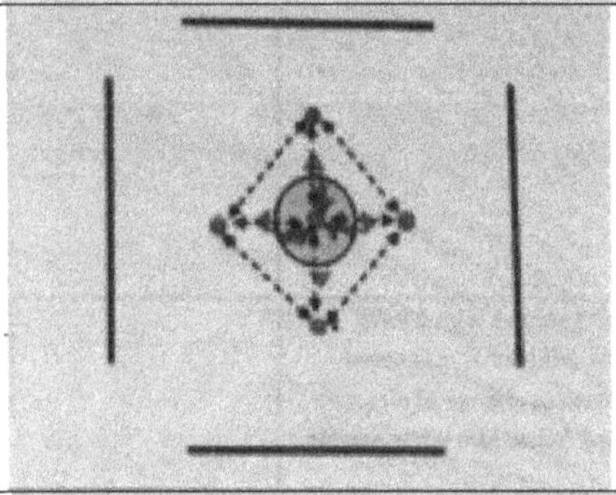	Los atacantes pasan el balón hacia fuera y tratan de pasar el balón al del medio. Si un defensor intercepta el balón trata de ponerlo detrás de la línea de atacantes.
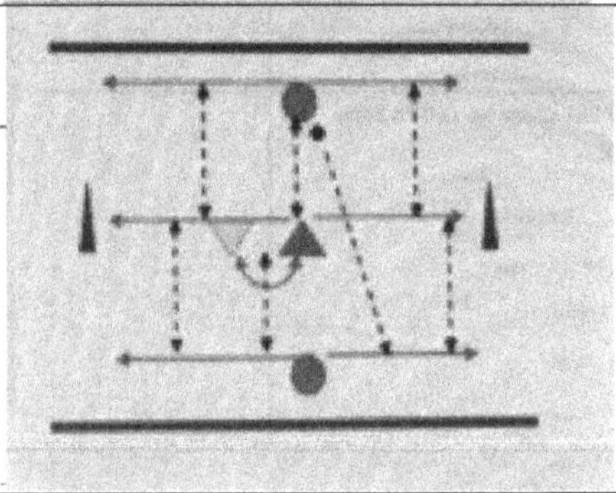	Atacantes y defensores pasan rápido y en movimiento. Los defensores intentan interceptar,
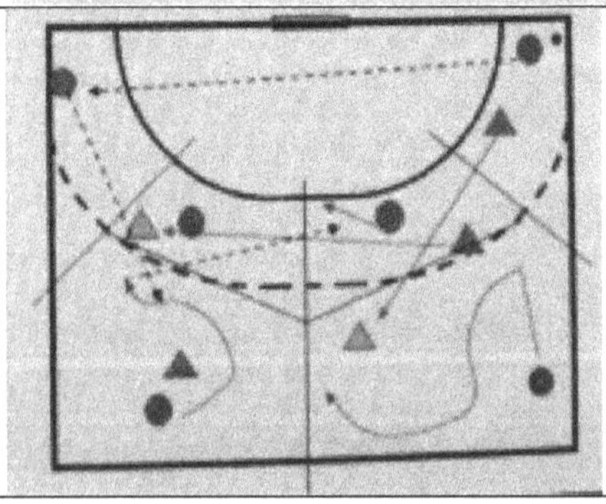	6 atacantes 3 defensores. Los atacantes intentan el máximo numero posibles de pases pero tienen solo 1 segundos de posesión si los defensas interceptan contraataque.

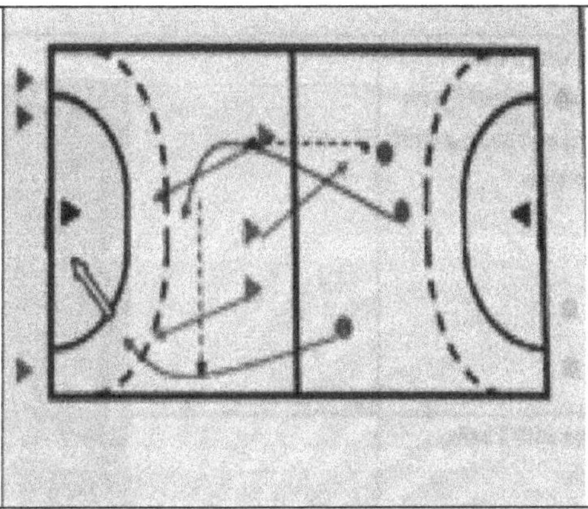	Partido cambio de equipo campo completo. Cambio después de cada gol
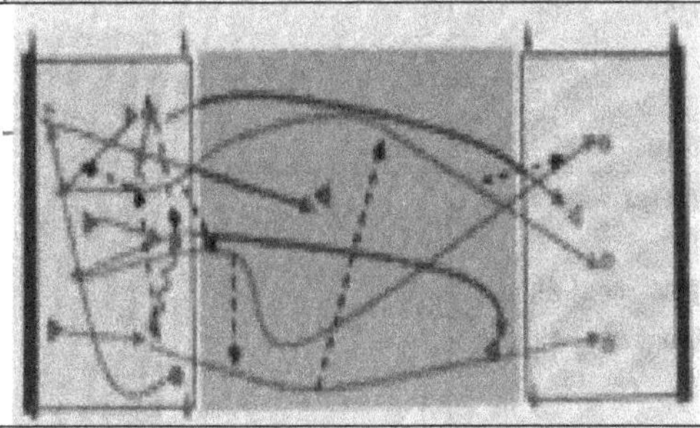	3 pases después defender la puerta zona 3:3 cuando interceptamos el balón debemos llagar al otro lado en 3 pases
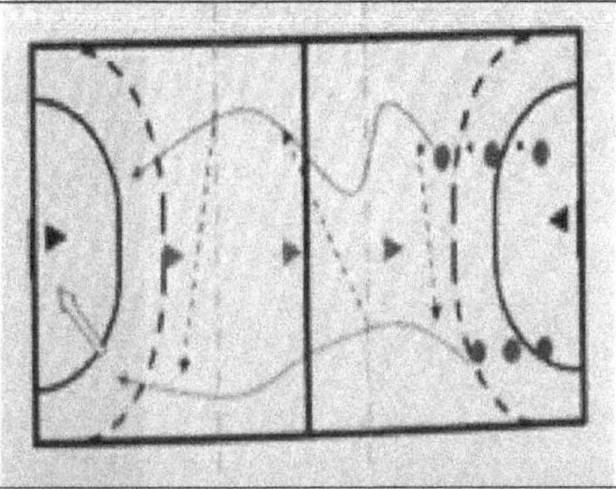	Superar 3 defensores transportando el balón Cada defensor defiende su zona sin botar
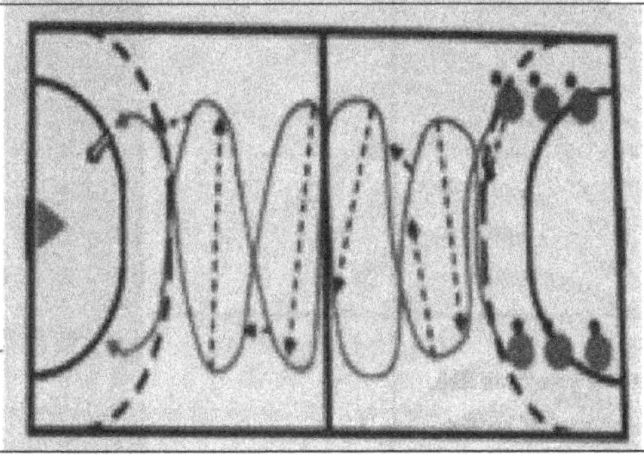	Grupo de 2 jugadores con 2 balones Progresión en máxima velocidad con continuos cruces y pases con 2 balones al mismo tiempo.

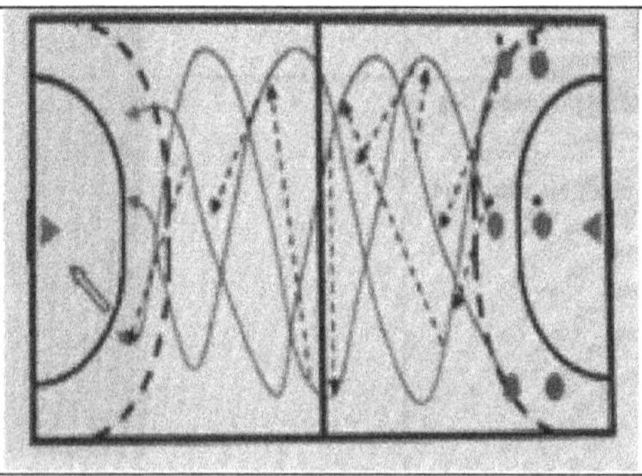	Grupo de 3 jugadores con 2 balones, lo mismo que el anterior.
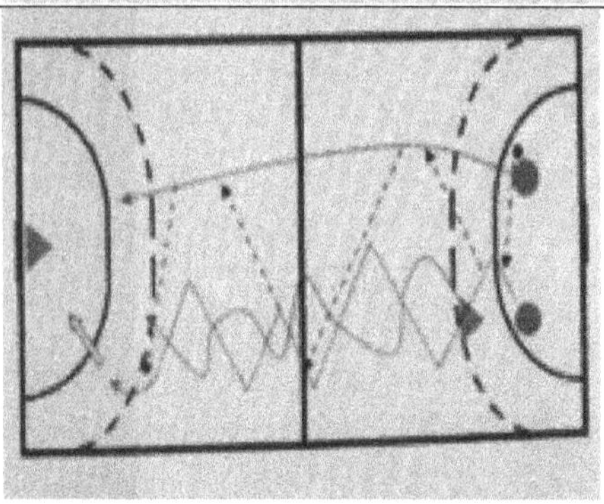	Grupo de 3 jugadores pasador, atacante y defensor. Progresar a máxima velocidad sin parar y desmarcándose sin regresar. Sin botar la defensa defiende solo el atacante y el pasador no tiene oposición.
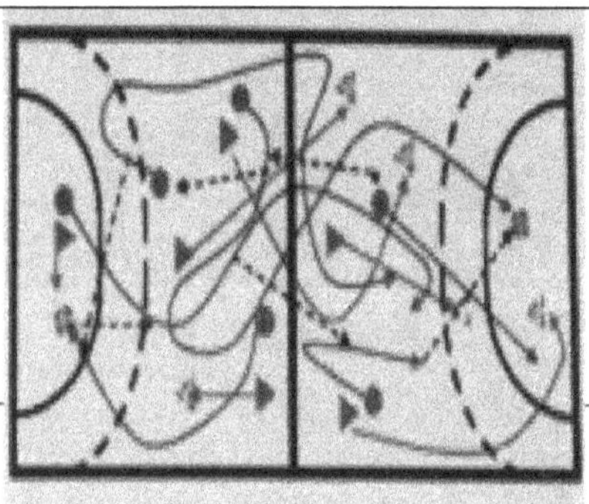	Juego de pases y recepciones Llevar el balón a diferentes partes de campo sin para y sin botar
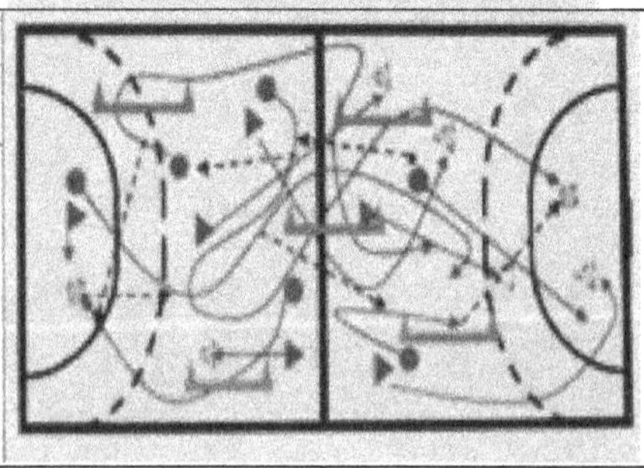	Pases y recepciones Transportar el balón a diferentes zonas y pasando por diferentes puertas

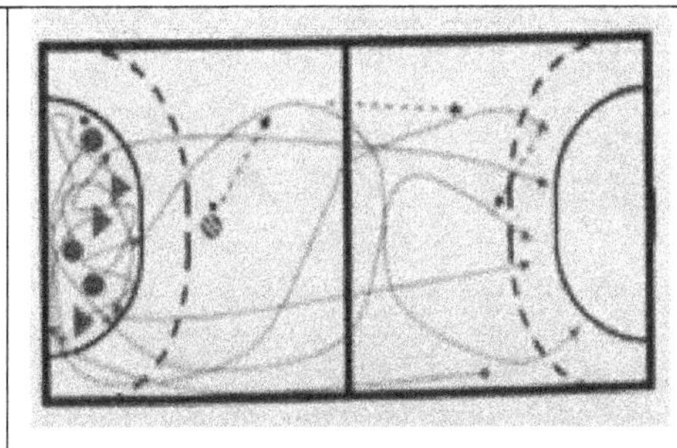

Pases en una zona y contraataques 3:3 o 4:4
Después de dar 5 pases pasamos al portero e iniciamos el contraataque. No bote, progresión 5 [ases en medio campo y luego contraataque.

ACKNOWLEDGMENTS

I'd like to thank my editor, Luis Diaz, for editing the Spanish version of this book. Your guidance and skill have allowed me to accomplish my dream of sharing my life's work as a player and coach of Handball.

To my English editors, Andrea Jasmin and Jasmine Wilson, thank you for lending your expertise in translating, editing, and formatting this book. I appreciate your commitment to bringing the English version of 50 Years in the Sport to light.